A Wonderful Flood of Light

A Wonderful Flood of Light

Neal A. Maxwell

Bookcraft
Salt Lake City, Utah

Library of Congress Catalog Card Number: 89–82331
ISBN 0–88494–728–9

2nd Printing, 1990

Printed in the United States of America

Contents

Acknowledgments

As always in such an undertaking as this, there are those to whom I must express my genuine appreciation.

Roy W. Doxey carefully checked scriptural references and made valuable suggestions. Liz Haglund checked early on for the flow of the manuscript, with helpful reactions. Stephen Robinson was kind enough to scrutinize scholarly references and related scriptures while making other insightful observations. Larry Skidmore pinpointed and verified my partially remembered quotations from earlier Brethren. These friends helped in ways which maximized my "free time" in July.

I especially thank Susan Jackson, who moved the manuscript through its several drafts.

Finally, my gratitude goes to George Bickerstaff and Cory Maxwell, who helped so much in the editing and publishing process.

This is not an official Church publication. Hence, even though I was helped in its preparation, I alone am responsible for the views it expresses.

Chapter One

"A Fresh View"

If people in what are referred to as Christian nations were asked what they think of Christ, for most of them the question would prove puzzling amid the secular din of our times. As life has grown more complex, the cares and perplexities and anxieties about things of the world have grown steadily more intrusive, demanding more and more of our resources, time, worry, and energy. Spiritual considerations come later, if at all. Yet faith is more than ever needed in what is at best a simmering disquiet as wars, terrorism, natural disasters, injustices, changing mores, aggressive materialism, political turbulence, and widespread human suffering all combine to produce an unprecedented uncertainty. To appreciate how relevant and responsive the Restoration is, it is necessary first to take at least a superficial measure of the consequences of the spiritual famine that preceded it (see Amos 8:11–12).

We are nearing a prophesied point in human history:

> And he answered them, and said, In the generation in
> which the times of the Gentiles shall be fulfilled, there shall be
> signs in the sun, and in the moon, and in the stars; and upon
> the earth distress of nations with perplexity, like the sea and
> the waves roaring. The earth also shall be troubled, and the
> waters of the great deep. (JST, Luke 21:25.)

As if the oppressive combination of the above factors,
"like the sea and the waves roaring," were not enough distrac-
tion, real commitment to the gospel of Jesus Christ is made
more difficult for many good people by certain stumbling
blocks that obscure the view of spiritual reality. These stumbling blocks can prevent not only initial belief but also deeper
belief. Even those on the strait and narrow path, if they are not
carefully renewed and refreshed, can become "wearied and
faint in [their] minds" (Hebrews 12:3).

Some sincerely ask hard questions that reflect the blocking
impediments. "If there is a God, and He is good, why does He
permit human suffering in the world?" Disciples may offer their
own variation of this question, as was expressed to Brigham
Young: "Why are [men] left alone and often sad?" (*Brigham
Young's Secretary's Journal*, January 28, 1857.)

Others, having at best only a partial view of the Fall, question the mercy and justice of God: "I cannot accept a Being
who would punish all mortals because of a mistake made by
their ancient ancestors in a garden thousands of years ago for
which their descendants obviously are not responsible."

In the face of such questions, those who want to believe in a
literal and resurrected Christ are often sincerely perturbed because of what seems to them to be a paucity of first-hand,
witnessing data thereto. One commentator wrote:

> The Gospel accounts, of course, offer clues about Jesus,
> but the Gospels are highly imperfect historical documents.
> They did not take final shape until the late first century, a full
> generation (or two) after the death of Jesus. . . . The Gospels
> were the work of people who already believed in Jesus as the
> risen Lord. . . . The Gospels almost certainly were not by any

of the twelve apostles and may or may not have been written by men named Matthew, Mark, Luke, and John, who may or may not have been alive at the time of Jesus, and who may or may not represent composites of many individual chroniclers. (Cullen Murphy, "Who Do Men Say That I Am?" *Atlantic Monthly*, December 1986, p. 38.)

This particular stone of stumbling is reminiscent of that which impeded some in an earlier period: "It is not reasonable that such a being as a Christ shall come . . . why will he not show himself unto us? . . . but in a land which is far distant . . . for we cannot witness with our own eyes. . . ." (Helaman 16:18–20). Thus as people ponder the human scene the fallout as to faith is considerable and varied.

Many contemporaries have concluded, just as did some anciently, that "when a man was dead, that was the end thereof" (Alma 30:18). Parallels in modern utterances include "No deity will save us; we must save ourselves" ("Humanist Manifesto II," *The Encyclopedia of American Religions: Religious Creeds*, J. Gordon Melton, ed. [Detroit: Gale Research Company, 1988], p. 641).

Not only have the cares and anxieties of the world had their impact, but special stumbling blocks exist because certain wrong and long traditions have taken their terrible toll on humankind.

Stephen Robinson has described an especially critical period in the history of Christianity out of which emerged serious doctrinal deficiencies that have plagued man ever since:

The second half of the first century . . . [to] the middle of the second century. . . . might be called the blind spot in Christian history, for it is here that the fewest primary historical sources have been preserved. We have good sources for New Testament Christianity; then the lights go out, so to speak, and we hear the muffled sounds of a great struggle. When the lights come on again a hundred or so years later, we find that someone has rearranged all the furniture and Christianity has become something very different from what it was in the beginning. That different entity can accurately be described as hellenized Christianity.

. . . Hellenization refers to the imposition of Greek culture and philosophy upon the cultures of the East. The result was a synthesis of East and West, a melting pot of popular culture that was virtually worldwide. In the realm of religion, however, synthesis means compromise, and when we speak in terms of the gospel, compromise with popular beliefs means apostasy from the truth.

. . . The Greeks' world-view eventually won, and Jewish Christianity was revised to make it more attractive and appealing to a Greek audience.

. . . In order to satisfy the Gentiles steeped in Greek philosophy, Christianity had to throw out the doctrines of an anthropomorphic God and the resurrection of the dead, or reinterpret them drastically. Denying or altering the doctrine of the resurrection of the dead is precisely what some Greek Christians at Corinth had done, and Paul responded against them forcefully in 1 Corinthians 15. . . .

In Doctrine and Covenants 86:3, the Lord identifies the whore, Babylon, as the apostate church: "After they [the Apostles] have fallen asleep the great persecutor of the church, the apostate, the whore, even Babylon, that maketh all nations to drink of her cup, in whose hearts the enemy, even Satan, sitteth to reign—behold he soweth the tares; wherefore, the tares choke the wheat and drive the church into the wilderness."

. . . It [the earliest apostate church] dethroned God in the church and replaced him with man by denying the principle of revelation and turning instead to human intellect. (Stephen E. Robinson, "Warring Against the Saints of God," *Ensign*, January 1988, pp. 38, 39.)

These and other serious errors of perception and assumption set in motion enormous theological and behavioral consequences which now wash over societies like eroding surf. Indeed there is much hindering history!

Religion has likewise been challenged by the emergence of certain scientific concepts, in some instances prompting needless rejection of religion in favor of secularism. One episode illustrates what can happen when, bereft of a fulness of scripture, a narrow mindset prevails over the viewing of "things as they really are" (Jacob 4:13).

After Galileo had turned his homemade telescope on the heavens for the first time in 1610, he wrote: "All the disputes which have tormented philosophers through so many ages are exploded at once by the irrefragable evidence of our eyes, and we are freed from wordy disputes upon this subject, for the Galaxy is nothing else but a mass of innumerable stars planted together in clusters. Upon whatever part of it you direct the telescope straightway a vast crowd of stars presents itself to view."

Yet Galileo, in June of 1633, was condemned to renounce, in the presence of a tribunal, the truths he had maintained as a result of his discoveries. The Christian "astronomy" that then triumphed, however, proved as unreliable as some of what then passed for "theology." As to the latter, for example, the Renaissance with its skeptical scholarship produced the argument, now generally accepted, that the Apostles' Creed "could not have been composed by the Twelve Apostles." (Daniel J. Boorstin, *The Discoverers* [New York: Random House, 1983], pp. 320, 577.)

Over the centuries as well as in recent decades, Christianity has suffered from a peculiar apostasy, an internal dilution. Speaking as of the year A.D. 101, one nineteenth-century historian even lamented, "The age of inspiration is over. . . . The last gleam of inspired wisdom and truth vanished from the earth with the beloved apostle's [John] gentle farewell" (Islay Burns, *The First Three Christian Centuries* [London: T. Nelson and Sons, 1884], p. 49).

Even fundamental, crucial concepts are in question. Today many, including some clerics, say "that the resurrection [of Jesus] was achieved not in the person of Jesus but only in the believing disciples, as it were. 'Resurrection' is then more a symbolic expression for the renewal of life for the disciples." (Quoted in Michael Harrington, *The Politics at God's Funeral* [New York: Holt, Rinehart and Winston, 1983], p. 164.)

Thus, in the foregoing pages, we see the urgency and relevance of the Restoration.

The restored gospel's answers to such vexing man-made problems are more than adequate even for those who "can no more than desire to believe" but who are at least willing to "give place" in their lives for God's words to grow there (Alma 32:27). Yet because of Christianity's dilution, even when God performs "a marvellous work and a wonder" (Isaiah 29:14; D&C 4:1) it is greeted with disdain and sometimes with hostility.

Flowing through the human condition too are many paradoxes and adverse linkages. As an example, the scriptures observe that, even among believers, "hearts are set so much upon the things of this world" that they have neither time nor disposition to learn vital lessons (D&C 121:35). Jesus foretold that in the latter days the love of many would wax cold (see Matthew 24:12; D&C 45:27). That condition of less love means that there is more fear (see 1 John 4:17; Moroni 8:16). And the more iniquity—another feature of our love-lessened age—the more human despair (see Moroni 10:22), which is a close associate of fear.

Yet another cyclic irony likewise emerges: The less faith among mortals, the less God works in certain ways among them (see 2 Nephi 27:23; Mormon 9:20). Moreover, where there is less faith there is also less repentance, for a true disciple always has "faith unto repentance" (Alma 34:15–17). An ironic and interactive combination has thus taken hold.

It is no wonder that responding to the rectifying, restored gospel, which requires a transformation of one's life, seems especially difficult in such an age. Words that are harsh-sounding and uninviting to moderns are woven into the fabric of the gospel—words such as *repentance* and *obedience*. In his "careful" conditioning process (see 2 Nephi 28:21) the adversary has seen to it that words like these give religion a bad name. In a world with a marketplace orientation such words have no soothing or appealing "marketing" dimension to them.

Practicing the concept of repentance involves a real wrenching: not only a "turning away" from sin and the world but also a "turning toward" God. It should be noted, however, that in the Greek *repentance* also means "a change of mind, i.e., a *fresh view* about God, about oneself, and about the world" (LDS Bible Dictionary, p. 760, italics added).[1] Given this latter affirmative connotation, it is easier to see why the Lord has said what He has said:

> Say nothing but repentance unto this generation (D&C 6:9).

> The thing which will be of the most worth unto you will be to declare repentance unto this people, that you may bring souls unto me, that you may rest with them in the kingdom of my Father (D&C 16:6).

When initiated by a realistic and fresh view of reality—of "things as they really are"—repentance can be embraced and hastened. This very process of personal progress was utilized by certain spiritual noblemen of antiquity: "Many . . . were ordained and became high priests of God; and it was on account of their exceeding faith and repentance, and their righteousness before God, they choosing to repent and work righteousness" (Alma 13:10).

In one degree or another, all of us need this precious process. We sorely need the spiritual stimulus of a "fresh view" of the great realities of the universe, a perspective persuasive and powerful enough to change and improve our lives. Otherwise, as Dom Pedro de Alcantara observed, we go on trying to change others instead of ourselves, so things do not improve but remain the same.

Powerful and persuasive reasons for the repentance of a fresh view are exactly what the Restoration provides through its wonderful flood of light. The restitution of all things brought with it a fresh view (the very one Adam had at the beginning)

---

1. "To change one's thinking" or even "reconsidering" are likewise renditions of the Greek verb and noun for repentance. In this book the sense of "changing one's mind" and of "a fresh view" will be emphasized.

about God, oneself, and the world. (Here we might note that divine disclosure often emphasizes the expansive; for example, certain ancient records were actually prepared precisely to "throw greater views on [the] gospel" [D&C 10:45].) Again, it is precisely what the world needs.

It is a sad fact that, lacking this fresh view, many fail to understand the true nature of full repentance. The Nephites at their worst provide an example of this failure: "But behold this my joy was vain, for their sorrowing was not unto repentance, because of the goodness of God; but it was rather the sorrowing of the damned, because the Lord would not always suffer them to take happiness in sin" (Mormon 2:13).

Repentance is a joy-producing process. In fact, it is impossible to find genuine happiness without it, because it is integral to that quality. Alma explained this to his son Corianton: "Men . . . have gone contrary to the nature of God; therefore, they are in a state contrary to the nature of happiness" (Alma 41:11). And in his impassioned speech to the unrepentant Nephites, the Lamanite prophet Samuel stressed the same theme: "Ye have sought all the days of your lives for that which ye could not obtain; . . . happiness in doing iniquity, which thing is contrary to the nature of that righteousness which is in our great and Eternal Head" (Helaman 13:38).

It follows that iniquity is perspective-shrinking, since it increasingly diminishes one's perception of redemptive reality. "If ye have no hope," Moroni wrote, "ye must needs be in despair; and despair cometh because of iniquity" (Moroni 10:22).

Historically and scripturally the Lord's prophets have preached this kind of message. One ancient and anxious prophet in particular yearned to help his fellowmen have the emancipating gospel view of things: "O that I were an angel," Alma exclaimed, "and could have the wish of mine heart, that I might go forth and speak with the trump of God, with a voice to shake the earth, and cry repentance unto every people!" (Alma 29:1.)

We can be sure that this prophet wanted to cry repentance, but to do so in the broadest and most liberating definition of that word. In his subsequent words, Alma speaks about the plan of redemption and the global nature of God's work.

A fresh view is not always welcomed, however; it can be jarring to those who are intensely set in their ways (see Isaiah 28:21). Even the remarkable Enoch was not welcomed by many of his contemporaries. Of him and his labors it was said anciently, "There is a strange thing in the land" (Moses 6:38). Isaiah's phrase "strange work" is amplified in Restoration scriptures. Fresh and striking truths were necessary so that mortals could "hear and know that which they have never considered" (D&C 101:94). Without such vision, people perish (see Proverbs 29:18).

Having described the Restoration as his "strange act," and "my strange work," the Lord indicated that it would go against the grain of much of society. Yet restitution of the unfamiliar, the uncommon, the unusual, and the unique would actually aid mortals by providing fresh, divine standards and help them in discerning between righteousness and wickedness, as God "poured out [His] Spirit upon all flesh." (D&C 95:4; 101:95.) With values otherwise shorn of true perspective, the inversions of certain of them become almost inevitable. Finally, evil can end up being called good, and good evil. (See Isaiah 5:20; 2 Nephi 15:20; Moroni 7:14.)

Even with the gospel's precious perspective and its provision of much-needed remedies, because of stumbling blocks and because of the cares and anxieties of the world comparatively few individuals will hear, and fewer still will accept, the unique message of the Restoration. This is not unlike the situation in which some of Galileo's friends reportedly refused to look through his telescope; they did not want to gain a fresh view of things. But the present spiritual case is an especially sad situation, for the restored gospel is composed of truths of the highest order of significance and of relevance. Its truths are about "things as they really are" (Jacob 4:13), providing just what is needed amid the boring hedonism or the "humdrum nihilism of everyday life" (*The Politics at God's Funeral*, p. 11). Most of all, however, the Restoration provides the vital doctrines, ordinances, authority, and organization essential to salvation and exaltation. No wonder the Lord desires "that all that will hear may hear" (D&C 1:11).

How we view ourselves, others, and the universe really does shape everything else! Our view of such strategic matters determines, among many other things, whether while on this planet we will act as concerned stewards or merely as transient pleasure-seekers and alien exploiters. A genuine world religion requires a world (not worldly) view—better still, a gospel with a galactic view!

Therefore, far from being no more than another collection of unusual theological points, the restored gospel is the key to human happiness! The fresh view is essential if one is to have a changed or new heart (see 1 Samuel 10:9; Alma 5:12-14, 26).

But God does not change our hearts against our wills. Change happens as a result of an inward awakening and of being stirred enough by a fresh view to "give place" and to change willingly (Alma 5:7; 32:27). Then a person can come to have sufficient faith to put his "trust in the true and living God." Moreover, it is to be a "mighty" and not merely a cosmetic change. The more "mighty" the change, the more clearly we see reality and the less we desire to do evil. (Mosiah 5:2, 7; Alma 5:13; 19:33.)

A fresh view both derives from and leads to an increasing belief in all the holy scriptures (see Helaman 15:7). As we progressively see by that light, our "minds become single to God" (D&C 88:68).

To go against the grain of society and to undergo such a mighty change requires a miracle. A special, spiritual stimulus was needed to provide the requisite fresh and powerful perspectives—something that would lift mankind (or at least lift the view of those with eyes to see) above the humdrum of the human condition. But the fresh view not only had to orient us in order to get us going in the right direction; it also had to provide sufficiently persuasive content to keep our gaze and our progress steady:

And now, my beloved brethren, after ye have gotten into this straight and narrow path, I would ask if all is done? Behold, I say unto you, Nay; for ye have not come thus far save it were by the word of Christ with unshaken faith in him, relying wholly upon the merits of him who is mighty to save.

Wherefore, ye must press forward with a steadfastness in Christ, having a perfect brightness of hope, and a love of God and of all men. Wherefore, if ye shall press forward, feasting upon the word of Christ, and endure to the end, behold, thus saith the Father: Ye shall have eternal life. (2 Nephi 31:19–20.)

Since feasting on the word of God has a "more powerful effect upon the minds of the people than . . . anything else" (Alma 31:5), the more of the word of God we have and act upon, the more we will press forward. Much spiritual energy is necessary for the marathon of discipleship.

As a great blessing, the word of God has been richly given to us in the Restoration. It provides a full and firm basis for real faith, especially in a world in which many are struggling to believe, and still others, bereft of a fresh view, have simply quit struggling! (See Alma 32:14; 2 Nephi 27:23.) Some still "run to and fro" in search of the word of the Lord (Amos 8:11–12), but others have quit running altogether. Such souls include disappointed idealists, resigned skeptics, and those driven to despair by the "old view."

To reemphasize, certain trends have "set the stage" for the Restoration, ensuring both its relevancy and its urgency, as shown in these observations:

Among the advanced races, the decline and ultimately the collapse of the religious impulse would leave a huge vacuum. The history of modern times is in great part the history of how that vacuum had been filled. . . . In place of religious belief, there would be secular ideology. (Paul Johnson, *Modern Times* [New York: Harper and Row, 1983], p. 48.)

Christianity would have to struggle for a hearing in a world where most would regard it not as untrue or even as unthinkable, but simply irrelevant. (Penelope Fitzgerald, *The Knox Brothers* [New York: Coward, McCann & Geoghegan, 1977], pp. 106-7.)

Some intelligent people, like much of mankind, find the way of faith difficult. Naturally, their ponderings and responses to mortality are varied, ranging from disbelief through tentativeness and hope and on to faith. In 1988 *Life* magazine asked some prominent people for their views on the meaning of life and why we are here, the results of which were published in the December 1988 issue. Selected answers follow below, showing the spread along the spectrum, with samples of the relevant responses the Restoration makes to the points under discussion.

Supreme Court Justice Harry Blackmun

But here we are. Not one of us asked to be here or had very much to do with his arrival. With our finite minds we cannot presume to know if there is a Purpose. We sense, however, the presence of something greater than we can comprehend, a force as yet unknown to us—perhaps ever to be unknown.

Restoration's Response

We will make an earth whereon these may dwell; and we will prove them herewith, to see if they will do all things whatsoever the Lord their God shall command them; and they who keep their first estate shall be added upon; and they who keep not their first estate shall not have glory in the same kingdom with those who keep their first estate; and they who keep their second estate shall have glory added upon their heads for ever and ever. (Abraham 3:24-26.)

When the morning stars sang together, and all the sons of God shouted for joy (Job 38:7).

For behold, this is my work and my glory—to bring to pass the immortality and eternal life of man (Moses 1:39).

And this is life eternal, that they might know thee the only true God, and Jesus Christ, whom thou hast sent (John 17:3).

Astronomer Frank Drake

There is no doubt that life will have developed in many places in our universe. Our own significance, our ultimate potential and our ensemble of possible destinies will be understood by finding and studying the other intelligent creatures of space. Thus a prime task is to seek out other intelligent civilizations and to share knowledge with them.

Restoration's Response

That by him, and through him, and of him, the worlds are and were created, and the inhabitants thereof are begotten sons and daughters unto God (D&C 76:24).

And thus there shall be the reckoning of the time of one planet above another, until thou come nigh unto Kolob, . . . which Kolob is set nigh unto the throne of God, to govern all those planets which belong to the same order as that upon which thou standest (Abraham 3:9).

And worlds without number have I created; and I also created them for mine own purpose; and by the Son I created them, which is mine Only Begotten. . . .
But only an account of this earth, and the inhabitants thereof, give I unto you. For behold, there are many worlds that have passed away by the word of my power. And there are many that now stand, and innumerable are they unto man; but all things are numbered unto me, for they are mine and I know them. . . .
And as one earth shall pass away, and the heavens thereof even so shall another come; and there is no end to my works, neither to my words. (Moses 1:33, 35, 38, italics added.)

Writer Charles Bukowski

For those who believe in God, most of the big questions are answered. But for those of us who can't readily accept the God formula, the big answers don't remain stone-written. We adjust to new conditions and discoveries. We are pliable. Love need not be a command or faith a dictum. I am my own God. We are here to unlearn the teachings of the church, state and our educational system. We are here to drink beer. We are here to kill war. We are here to laugh at the odds and live our lives so well that Death will tremble to take us.

Restoration's Response

They seek not the Lord to establish his righteousness, but every man walketh in his own way, and after the image of his own god, whose image is in the likeness of the world (D&C 1:16).

Writer D. M. Thomas

Astronomer Fred Hoyle observed that it was no more likely that our world has evolved out of chaos than that a hurricane, blowing through a junkyard, should create a Boeing.

Looking at certain people who have or had strong religious feeling, I am often impressed by a depth of spirituality that "the good atheist" very rarely has. I am thinking of people like Mother Teresa, Carl Jung, Anna Akhmatova, Boris Pasternak. The last two are great poets; and it is not easy to find poets who have no religious concept. If in doubt, I have always felt, trust the poets.

Restoration's Response

Poets truly can inspire and inform, but they do not presume to declare doctrine. Even William Wordsworth's evocative imagery about our coming here "trailing clouds of glory" has those limitations. Wordsworth explained his use of this pre-existent imagery thus: "A pre-existent state has entered into the popular creeds of many nations. . . . I took hold of the notion of pre-existence as having sufficient foundation in humanity for authorizing me to make for my purpose the best use of it I could as a poet." Wordsworth said such a belief "is far too shadowy a notion to be recommended to faith. . . . Though the idea is not advanced in revelation, there is nothing there to contradict it, and the fall of man presents an analogy in its favour." (Alfred Noyes, ed., *English Romantic Poetry and Prose* [New York: Oxford University Press, 1956], pp. 327–28.)

A revelation of which Wordsworth was unaware came through the Prophet Joseph while the poet was still alive. "Man was also in the beginning with God. Intelligence, or the light of truth, was not created or made, neither indeed can be." (D&C 93:29.)

Into such a setting as the above comments represent, with mortals spread across a spectrum, the wonderful flood of light from heaven has come with the fresh view. The glorious and much-needed perspectives of the Restoration mean that "faith also might increase in the earth" (D&C 1:21). It was so miraculous and so urgently needed. Divinely given revelation thus provides a basis for the changing of minds. Thus the gospel of repentance leads not only to the forgiveness of sins but also to becoming converted to the Lord's plan, with the comprehensiveness, uniqueness, and brightness of its perspective. Otherwise the great realities concerning mankind would go unseen, unbelieved, and unheeded.

Chapter Two

"A MIRACULOUS MIRACLE"

The prophetic words of Isaiah 29:14 concerning the remarkable Restoration are fully justified. It was and is a "marvellous work and a wonder," or, as those words read when rendered in Hebrew, "a miraculous miracle"! God, who is not given to exaggeration, reflected upon the creation of this beautiful and spectacular earth as "very good." Yet through Isaiah and in revelations given to Joseph Smith in February 1829, and repeatedly thereafter, He announced the coming of the "marvelous work." (See Genesis 1:31; D&C 4:1; 6:1; 11:1; 12:1; 18:44.) The phrases "marvellous work and a wonder" and the "miraculous miracle" are deliberately redundant. And the restored gospel, including the Book of Mormon, *is* the prophesied "miraculous miracle."

The perspective-yielding truths of the Restoration did not come by research, debate, or discussion, nor by communiques from councils. Direct, divine revelation was required, and precisely for the reasons Jacob gave: "Behold, great and marvelous are the works of the Lord. How unsearchable are the depths of the mysteries of him; and it is impossible that man should find out all his ways. And no man knoweth of his ways save it be revealed unto him; wherefore, brethren, despise not the revelations of God." (Jacob 4:8.)

We cannot determine by using radio telescopes, for instance, that there is a plan of salvation operating in the universe, helpful as radio telescopes are for astrophysical purposes. Salvational truths are obtainable only by revelation.

The faith-yielding truths flowing from the "miraculous miracle" have come in rich abundance, in "good measure," like a harvest basket whose contents are "pressed down, and shaken together, and running over" (Luke 6:38). In fact, as Elder Jeffrey R. Holland has pointed out, more books or pages of scripture have come to us through Joseph Smith than from any other prophet—more even than from Moses, Luke, Paul, and Mormon combined! (Letter to author from Jeffrey R. Holland, February 18, 1986.)

Many more scriptural writings will yet come to us, including those of Enoch (see D&C 107:57), all of the writings of the Apostle John (see Ether 4:16), the records of the lost tribes of Israel (see 2 Nephi 29:13), and the approximately two-thirds of the Book of Mormon plates that were sealed: "And the day cometh that the words of the book which were sealed shall be read upon the house tops; and they shall be read by the power of Christ; and all things shall be revealed unto the children of men which ever have been among the children of men, and which ever will be even unto the end of the earth" (2 Nephi 27:11). Today we carry convenient quadruple combinations of the scriptures, but one day, since more scriptures are coming, we may need to pull little red wagons brimful with books.

Speaking of our feelings in mortality about life beyond the veil, C. S. Lewis observed: "We cannot mingle with the splendours we see. But all the leaves of the New Testament are rustling with the rumour that it will not always be so." How much more is it the case when, through the Restoration, the New Testament is joined by hundreds more leaves which are rustling resoundingly! If, as was said of great secular literature, "My own eyes are not enough for me; I will see through those of others. . . . I will become a thousand men and yet remain myself"—how much more true this ought to be as regards holy literature! (James T. Como, ed., *C. S. Lewis at the Breakfast Table, and Other Reminiscences* [New York: Macmillan, 1979], pp. 34, xxxiii.) Better still, let us, like the servant of Elisha, have our eyes opened (see 2 Kings 6:15–17).

Prophecies have been fulfilled by the Restoration, a season in human history in which there would be a "restitution of all things, which God hath spoken by the mouth of all his holy prophets since the world began" (Acts 3:21). An essential part of that restitution was the restoration of priesthood keys. This made it possible for the Lord's Church to be "established in the last days for the restoration of his people, as he has spoken by the mouth of his prophets" (D&C 84:2). As this scripture shows, the concept of restitution or restoration was well understood and expressed by ancient prophets. Though initially Joseph Smith would not have been keenly conscious of this theme, as the great prophet of the last dispensation he certainly was later in his ministry.

As to that word *dispensation*, The Church of Jesus Christ of Latter-day Saints is in the unique position of knowing that there were various gospel dispensations prior to that of Jesus in the meridian of time, and that they linked all past prophets with Jesus and with the latter-day restoration. The coming forth of revelation and ancient records, in fact, teaches us that the gospel and its ordinances were upon the earth at the time of Adam. "And thus the Gospel began to be preached, from the beginning, being declared by holy angels sent forth from the presence of God, and by his own voice, and by the gift of the Holy Ghost. And thus all things were confirmed unto Adam, by an holy ordinance, and the Gospel preached, and a decree sent forth, that it should be in the world, until the end thereof; and thus it was." (Moses 5:58–59.)

Consistent with man's agency, down through the centuries since Adam's day God has done all he could to make available to his children the gospel of salvation, with its focus on the power of the Savior's atonement. The Prophet Joseph Smith commented: "We may conclude, that though there were different dispensations, yet all things which God communicated to His people were calculated to draw their minds to the great object, and to teach them to rely upon God alone as the author of their salvation, as contained in His law." (Joseph Smith, *Teachings of the Prophet Joseph Smith*, sel. Joseph Fielding Smith [Salt Lake City: Deseret Book, 1976], p. 61. Hereafter cited as *Teachings*.)

Ideas taught in the restored gospel are often reflected in other cultures—in the literature, philosophy, folklore, and religion of peoples and places around the globe. Elder Joseph F. Smith at once explained this situation and underscored the uniqueness of Latter-day Saint understanding and of our position in the world of religion:

> Undoubtedly the knowledge of this law [of sacrifice] and of other rites and ceremonies was carried by the posterity of Adam into all lands, and continued with them, more or less pure, to the flood, and through Noah, who was a "preacher of righteousness," to those who succeeded him, spreading out into all nations and countries, Adam and Noah being the first of their dispensations to receive them from God. What wonder, then, that we should find relics of Christianity, so to speak, among the heathens and nations who know not Christ, and whose histories date back beyond the days of Moses, and even beyond the flood, independent of and apart from the records of the Bible. (Joseph F. Smith, in *Journal of Discourses* 15: 325.)

It is clear that the dispersion, diffusion, and distortion of gospel truths has left fragments of the faith in various religions and cultures throughout the world. Many see in this an attempt by man to make his own god and religion in the absence of real ones. Rather than such similarities being evidence against the existence of God, however, these refracted truths bear witness of the initial wholeness which existed in the beginning with Adam.

Besides the diffusion of gospel teachings, there developed also some imitation of them: "Pharaoh, being a righteous man, established his kingdom and judged his people wisely and justly all his days, seeking earnestly to imitate that order established by the fathers in the first generations, in the days of the first patriarchal reign, even in the reign of Adam" (Abraham 1:26).

Being either unaware or unaccepting of truths revealed through the Restoration, many think that Christianity had no existence prior to Jesus' mortal messiahship in the meridian of time. If that were so, how would we explain Christian teachings found in documents predating the earthly ministry of Jesus? Was Jesus simply a charismatic eclectic who incorporated earlier ideas into His "new" religion? Was He something less than the sole originator of Christianity? Was he a mere collector and reproducer of other men's ideas?

Without the Restoration we would be left with a Jesus reduced in perceived significance by skepticism and pushed from full view by the sheer weight of human history. As it is, through the renewing Restoration scriptures we learn that over the sweep of the centuries divine dispensing has occurred as circumstances and faith have allowed: "And they began from that time forth [Adam's day] to call on his name; therefore God conversed with men, and made known unto them the plan of redemption, which had been prepared from the foundation of the world; and this he made known unto them according to their faith and repentance and their holy works" (Alma 12:30).

The phrases "plan of redemption" (as in the above verse), "plan of salvation," and "plan of happiness" appear multiple times in the Restoration scriptures. Knowledge of God's plan was clearly one of the "plain and precious things" which needed to be restored in a disbelieving and skeptical world, a world in which apostasy had taken its toll (see 1 Nephi 13:39–40). A specific instance is seen in the history of ancient Israel: "And the Lord said unto Moses, Hew thee two other tables of stone, like unto the first, and I will write upon them also, the words of the law, according as they were written at the first on the tables which thou brakest; but it shall not be according to the first, for I will take away the priesthood out of their midst; therefore my holy order, and the ordinances thereof, shall not go before them" (JST, Exodus 34:1).

As an offset to some of the effects of apostasy, throughout history the Lord has given as much light to various nations and people as their spiritual condition permitted (see Alma 29:8; 12:9; John 16:12; 3 Nephi 26:10; Ether 4:7). In this connection Joseph Smith observed:

> It is reasonable to suppose that man departed from the first teachings, or instructions which he received from heaven in the first age, and refused by his disobedience to be governed by them. Consequently, he formed such laws as best suited his own mind, or as he supposed, were best adapted to his situation. But that God has influenced man more or less since that time in the formation of law for his benefit we have no hesitancy in believing; for, . . . being the source of all good, every just and equitable law was in a greater or less degree influenced by Him. (*Teachings*, p. 57.)

All the fallings away in the various dispensations had been taken into account beforehand in the Lord's plans. Those plans pointed to the time of full reestablishment, "strange" as that latter-day act would seem to those by then steeped in other traditions (see Isaiah 28:21; D&C 101:94-95; 95:4). To quote the Prophet again: "The great Jehovah contemplated the whole of the events connected with the earth, pertaining to the plan of salvation, before it rolled into existence, or ever "the morning stars sang together" for joy; the past, the present, and the future were and are, with Him, one eternal "now"; He knew . . . the depth of iniquity that would be connected with the human family, . . . and has made ample provision for their redemption" (*Teachings*, p. 220).

The "ample provision" God has made for the human family surely includes "the miraculous miracle" spoken of by all the holy prophets since the world began!

Among the transcendent things restored as a part of the "restitution of all things" were the following:

The holy priesthood and its keys
The initiatory ordinances
The holy endowment
The true order of prayer
Baptism for the dead
The sealing power

Most striking to contemplate is this fact: When the lad Joseph Smith went into the Sacred Grove he did not go seeking these transcendent things, for he knew not of them. He went merely to learn which church to join!

One of the things achieved by the Restoration is a fresh view of the most transcendent being—Jesus Christ. This view, this flood of light, magnifies Jesus in a doubting world. There are those who regard Jesus as a "great moral teacher." He surely was that—history's *greatest* moral teacher, in fact—but He was much more! He was and is not just "one of the prophets" but Lord of all the prophets (see Matthew 16:14; John 7:40). Moreover, he was the preeminent Shepherd to all the Old Testament prophets. John recorded: "Jesus said unto them, Verily, verily, I say unto you, Before Abraham was, I am" (John 8:58). The Savior also said: "For had ye believed Moses, ye would have believed me: for he wrote of me." (John 5:46; see also 1 Corinthians 10:4; Hebrews 1:1-3; Colossians 1:15-18.)

Jesus links all the prophets together, just as was indicated on the Mount of Transfiguration when Moses and Elias were there to join Jesus and Peter, James, and John (see Matthew 17:1-8). A similar linkage occurred later too, in the Kirtland temple, when Jesus was there with His modern prophet, Joseph Smith, and Moses, Elias, and Elijah (see D&C 110).

The Prophet Joseph Smith taught that Moses received the holy endowment on a mountain top. President Joseph Fielding Smith expressed the further opinion that when sacred priesthood keys were passed on the Mount of Transfiguration (see *Teachings*, p. 158), the holy endowment was given to Peter, James, and John (see Joseph Fielding Smith, *Doctrines of Salva-*

tion, comp. Bruce R. McConkie, 3 vols. [Salt Lake City: Book-craft, 1954–56], 2:165).

This participation of prophets and dispensations, as noted earlier, is one of the unique features of the Restoration. Jesus even calls the Old Testament prophets "my prophets" (see 3 Nephi 1:13). It is all part of the "miraculous miracle" which magnifies Jesus:

> We knew of Christ, and we had a hope of his glory many hundred years before his coming; and not only we ourselves had a hope of his glory, but also all the holy prophets which were before us (Jacob 4:4).

> And now behold, Moses did not only testify of these things, but also all the holy prophets, from his days even to the days of Abraham. . . . It [was] shown unto the people, a great many thousand years before his coming, that even redemption should come unto them. (Helaman 8:16, 18.)

Evidence for this linkage of prophets and dispensations is not abundantly present in the Bible, because some of the "plain and precious things" were "kept back" or "taken away" from what became that book (1 Nephi 13:34, 39, 40). Part of the flood of light that accompanied the Restoration was the return of these lost truths. Naturally, many of them concern the central figure in the life of mankind.

In Restoration scriptures, in fact, Jesus Christ is clearly and definitively revealed to be the Lord of the universe, the creator of myriad worlds, a fact that is sparsely noted in the Bible (only three verses—John 1:3; Hebrews 1:2; 11:3):

> By him, and through him, and of him, the worlds are and were created, and the inhabitants thereof are begotten sons and daughters unto God (D&C 76:24).

> And worlds without number have I created; and I also created them for mine own purpose; and by the Son I created them, which is mine Only Begotten (Moses 1:33).

The worlds were made by him; men were made by him; all things were made by him, and through him, and of him (D&C 93:10).

Clearly, then, Latter-day Saints cannot regard Jesus as merely a "great moral teacher," or merely a "minor prophet," or even as only a "major prophet," significant to humans as each of these functions is. Rather, because of the Restoration, we understand Jesus' role in which, under the direction of the Father, He was the creator of this and other worlds. We worship a multi-planet God!

We cannot comprehend it all, of course. We do not know how many inhabited worlds there are, or where they are. But certainly we are not alone. This is a universe of spiritual order, in which "Kolob is set nigh unto the throne of God, to govern all those planets which belong to the same order as that upon which thou standest" (Abraham 3:9).

Our planet-home, we are told, is not impressive as to its size or location: "The earth is a medium-sized planet orbiting around an average star in the outer suburbs of an ordinary spiral galaxy, which is itself only one of about a million million galaxies in the observable universe" (Stephen W. Hawking, *A Brief History of Time* [New York: Bantam Books, 1988] p. 126). Lacking the concept of the divine design which abounds in the fresh view made possible by the Restoration's wonderful flood of light, some say we live in "an unsponsored universe," in an "empire of chance" (Bertrand Russell, "A Free Man's Worship," in *Mysticism and Logic and Other Essays* [London: George Allen and Unwin Ltd., 1951], p. 57).

Looking back to the time of Galileo we note that some biblical scriptures support his view as based on his discoveries. Isaiah, for example, wrote that the Lord created this earth not in vain, but to be inhabited (see Isaiah 45:18). Paul twice noted that Christ created other worlds as well as this one (see Hebrews 1:2; 11:3). John declared that Christ, under the Father's direction, created "all things" (John 1:3). Presumably these scriptural declarations were available at least to the educated in Galileo's day. Yet many, having not seen and/or having not believed these few scriptures, followed the philosophies of men and wrongly assumed that this earth was a solitary thing —even the center of the universe.

In the restored gospel, however, we are blessed with a richness of understanding—both confirmation of and much elaboration concerning what John and Paul wrote. Restoration revelations tell us much more about "things as they really are" (Jacob 4:13; see also Moses 1:32–35; D&C 76:24).

The restored gospel of Jesus Christ thus brings a greater illumination that corrects fundamental errors of assumption and perception about man and the universe. But only for those who will entertain the light which makes it clear that we live amid divine design in the enveloping empire of Elohim!

Hyrum Smith, who was part of the unfolding of the Restoration, had this precious perspective:

> The God of the armies of Israel is a wise God, He comprehended the end from the beginning, and adapted his plans, his designs and teachings to the peculiar wants, the local situation, the exigencies of mankind, and the present and future good of the human family; and everything that He has designed to notice by way of instruction to the children of men is given by infinite wisdom . . . beyond the comprehension of man in his present state. (Hyrum Smith, in Joseph E. Cardon and Samuel O. Bennion, *Testimonies of the Divinity of The Church of Jesus Christ of Latter-day Saints* [Independence: Zion's Printing and Publishing, 1930], p. 34. Hereafter cited as *Book of Testimonies*.)

Lack of such perspective about such great realities has led to confusion about man and the universe in many minds and hearts. Without access to a fulness of scriptures, people substituted deliberation for revelation. It was as the Savior said in denouncing the hypocritical lawyers: "For ye have taken away the key of knowledge, the fulness of the scriptures" (JST, Luke 11:53).

In the meridian of time, the misreading of the nature and role of Jesus Christ caused severe problems for some. Jesus had invited his hearers to come to him and satisfy their spiritual thirst. "Many of the people therefore, when they heard this saying, said, Of a truth this is the Prophet. Others said, This is the Christ. But some said, Shall Christ come out of Galilee? Hath not the scripture said, That Christ cometh of the seed of David, and out of the town of Bethlehem, where David was? So there was a division among the people because of him." (John 7:40–43.)

Where the Messiah was to be born was clear in Micah's prophecy (Micah 5:2), but what of where He would be reared? "And he came and dwelt in a city called Nazareth: that it might be fulfilled which was spoken by the prophets, He shall be called a Nazarene" (Matthew 2:23). In fact, it was foretold that his mother would be a Nazarene: "And it came to pass that I looked and beheld the great city of Jerusalem, and also other cities. And I beheld the city of Nazareth; and in the city of Nazareth I beheld a virgin, and she was exceedingly fair and white." (1 Nephi 11:13.)

Jesus was born in Bethlehem just as Micah had prophesied, but he was also reared in a city called Nazareth that he might be a Nazarene. The "stumbling" of his contemporaries over Jesus' identity occurred because people lacked the fulness of the scriptures and twisted the scriptures they did possess!

In later centuries, in debates between various factions, similar stumbling was caused by the same lack of fulness. These deliberations produced creeds which demonstrated the lack of a completeness that can be supplied only by revelation.

Some time after the deaths of the Apostles, confusion arose concerning the nature of the Father and the Son. To settle the issues and compose a creed, the Emperor Constantine convened the great Council of Nicaea (A.D. 325). Here is a scholar's description of a portion of that council:

> The closing speech of the mightiest of councils. . . . was delivered, fittingly, by the emperor, "who was first to bear witness to the correctness of the creed," according to Eusebius in a letter to his own flock, ". . . and he urged everyone to come to the same opinion and sign the statement of dogmas

and to agree with each other by signing a statement to which but a single term had been added—the word, *homoousion.*" The emperor then proceeded to explain with much technical language that word (which had been agreed on in committee) and the final verdict that the thing was really incomprehensible. "So in such a manner," Eusebius concludes, "our most wise and most devout (*eusebes,* blessed) Emperor *philosophized*; and the Bishops by way of explaining the *homoousios* prepared the following statement." (Hugh Nibley, *The World and the Prophets* [Salt Lake City: Deseret Book, 1987], pp. 46–47.)

Here we see the bankruptcy of beliefs which are a blend of philosophy and scripture instead of being derived from revelation. It is instructive to compare the above methods and results with those of the Nephite Twelve when the latter were perplexed on an important matter (see 3 Nephi 27:1–8).

Clearly Latter-day Saints need not be concerned about their Christianity being judged by conformity with the blended creeds. What we should prefer, of course, is to be judged by how we live and by what we believe concerning the Lord Jesus Christ, who is a Savior magnified mightily because of the added truths about Him that flow from the miraculous miracle.

Significantly, the miraculous miracle opened with a vision of the Father and the Son, when Joseph Smith "saw two Personages, whose brightness and glory defy all description, standing above [him] in the air." (Joseph Smith—History 1:17.) The vision Joseph Smith had of "two Personages," one of whom introduced the other as His Son, provided the truth needed to end creedal confusion as to the nature of the Father and the Son.

It is a very important fact that knowing the truth about Deity helps us to understand our own identity. "If men do not comprehend the character of God," the Prophet said, "they do not comprehend themselves" (*Teachings,* p. 343).

Comprehending God's character and Jesus' can be a needed spur to our own spiritual achievement; this understanding can help to increase faith in the earth (D&C 1:21). By way of example, the doctrines of premortality and foreordination overturn other false doctrines or traditions that suggest our spirits were created out of nothing.

Confirmation, elaboration, and clarification of key biblical scriptures also come through the Restoration. Compare, for instance, two accounts of some of the Lord's words at His second coming:

> And one shall say unto him, What are these wounds in thine hands? Then he shall answer, Those with which I was wounded in the house of my friends. (Zechariah 13:6.)

> And then shall the Jews look upon me and say: What are these wounds in thine hands and in thy feet?

> Then shall they know that I am the Lord; for I will say unto them: These wounds are the wounds with which I was wounded in the house of my friends. I am he who was lifted up. I am Jesus that was crucified. I am the Son of God.

> And then shall they weep because of their iniquities; then shall they lament because they persecuted their king. (D&C 45:51–53.)

Zechariah may have been constrained from saying more; or alternatively, some of what he said may have become lost from the biblical record. In any case, the miraculous miracle has brought us more about the marvelous events surrounding the second coming of the Savior.

We can make the same comparison as regards how we should live and what we should strive to become: "And [Jesus] said, Verily I say unto you, Except ye be converted, and become as little children, ye shall not enter into the kingdom of heaven" (Matthew 18:3).

What specifically is meant by this crucial quality of becoming "as little children"? We get some information in the New Testament, but we get a fulness in the Restoration, as in these words from King Benjamin's mighty sermon: ". . . and becometh as a child, submissive, meek, humble, patient, full of love, willing to submit to all things which the Lord seeth fit to inflict upon him, even as a child doth submit to his father" (Mosiah 3:19).

In contrast to the skepticism and disbelief of our times, the Restoration brings rich reassurance, including vital truths about the purposes of mortal life and the meaning of human existence. Isaiah wrote: "For thus saith the Lord that created the heavens; God himself that formed the earth and made it; he hath established it, he created it not in vain, he formed it to be inhabited" (Isaiah 45:18).

Isaiah thus tells us that this earth was purposefully formed to be inhabited. But why? The Book of Mormon confirms: "Behold, the Lord hath created the earth that it should be inhabited; and he hath created his children that they should possess it" (1 Nephi 17:36).

But the modern restoration of words from ancient revelations goes much further. The Lord summarized his purpose as follows: "For behold, this is my work and my glory—to bring to pass the immortality and eternal life of man" (Moses 1:39). And much of Abraham's vision of premortality, restored through the Prophet Joseph Smith, focused sharply on God's purpose for the created earth of Isaiah's and Nephi's expressions—the proving ground for His spirit children: "And we will prove them herewith, to see if they will do all things whatsoever the Lord their God shall command them" (Abraham 3:25).

Yes, this mortal existence had definite tutorial purposes, as Mormon perceived in commenting on the trials of a group of faithful disciples: "Nevertheless the Lord seeth fit to chasten his people; yea, he trieth their patience and their faith" (Mosiah 23:21). The directions concerning the need to understand life as a proving and tutoring experience are in the Holy Bible but are less than fully affirmed. A similar lack of fulness is there as to the fall of Adam, the infinite atonement, the Council in Heaven, and Lucifer's fall. These essential doctrines, only partially described in the Bible, are therefore sometimes either discounted or ignored. Latter-day Saints are greatly blessed to have these critical truths amplified in Restoration scriptures.

Restored too is the Old Testament's theme of remembrance, as the ancient view becomes part of the fresh view we now have. "Remember the days of old, consider the years of many generations: ask thy father, and he will shew thee; thy elders, and they will tell thee. When the most High divided to the nations their inheritance, when he separated the sons of Adam, he set the bounds of the people according to the number of the children of Israel." (Deuteronomy 32:7–8.)

Enoch, about whom there are only seven verses in the Bible, becomes a major figure in Restoration scripture. There are eighteen times as many column inches about Enoch in the Restoration scriptures than we have in the few verses on him in the Bible. Those scriptures not only contain greater quantity but also greater quality—dozens of verses containing new material about Enoch on which the Bible is silent. (Robert J. Matthews, letter to author dated August 12, 1988.) We would not even know about the city of Enoch were it not for the richness of the Restoration scriptures about him and his outstanding ministry.

Much more fully revealed by the Restoration, too, is the eventual return of the lost tribes of Israel with their scriptures (see 2 Nephi 29:12–14; D&C 110:11). It is the same regarding the gathering of the Jews and their return to the Holy Land (see 2 Nephi 9:2; 25:15–18; D&C 133:13, 35).

Although we have here touched on many matters that are illumined by the Restoration, actually as a church we are still "inventorying" the contents of its overflowing harvest basket. Clearly, other possibilities await a more full assessment and a careful pondering.

Mankind needs the truth about the things we have been discussing, in order to have faith in God. The Restoration ushered in truths highly essential to the increase of faith (see Acts 3:19). No wonder, therefore, that we are urged to move forward "in so great a cause" (D&C 128:20).

We believe the Book of Mormon because of the witness of the Spirit and because of the book's impressive internal evidences. We do not rely overly much on external evidences, but still it is good to be aware of it as corroborating information comes along.

The Book of Mormon, indeed a marvelous work and a wonder, is rich beyond our present appreciation. Examples are the apparent presence of Jewish festivals in the Book of Mormon, and extensive and precise chiasmus. When Joseph was translating the record, he could not have known of such things. Once he even inquired of Emma as to whether there were walls around Jerusalem! He simply did not know.

The demographic impact of the Restoration was very small in the beginning, but it is crescendoing in the last decade of the twentieth century and will soon flow and spread into the twenty-first century. Increasingly we shall see the Lord's words being fulfilled: "Righteousness and truth will I cause to sweep the earth as with a flood" (Moses 7:62). And again, "But first let my army become very great, and let it be sanctified before me" (D&C 105:31). The kingdom will also be constrained by conditions. Looking ahead two and a half millennia in vision, Nephi wrote: "I beheld that the church of the Lamb, . . . the saints of God were also upon all the face of the earth; and their dominions upon all the face of the earth were small, because of the wickedness" (1 Nephi 14:12). Regrettably, Satan's power would expand as the Lord's kingdom grew. Said Brigham Young: "It was revealed to me in the commencement of this Church, that the Church would spread, prosper, grow and extend, and that in proportion to the spread of the Gospel among the nations of the earth, so would the power of Satan rise (in *Journal of Discourses* 13:280).

And it all began with a lad who simply wanted to know which church to join!

There is a rhythm to the Restoration not unlike the sequence portrayed in the Lord's parable of the great supper. All nations are to be invited. The comparatively rich come first, and then, in a special demonstration of the Lord's power, the poor (see D&C 58:9–11). Just dawning on most Church members is the demanding reality that we must finally take the gospel to the multitudes of poor and the otherwise deprived upon the earth. The challenges will be many and vexing. Yet it will be as during His mortal messiahship, when "the common people heard [Jesus] gladly" (Mark 12:37).

We will see prophecies fulfilled, some of which cannot be fulfilled without accompanying dissonance. For instance, President Brigham Young observed of constraining political conditions in certain nations that "the Lord will yet revolutionize those nations until the door will be opened and the gospel will be preached to all" (in *Journal of Discourses* 12:256).

God will bring to pass his purposes in His own natural ways, while for us as a people and as individuals it remains to be wise as serpents and harmless as doves (Matthew 10:16).

There are many ways in which the freshening miraculous miracle can be appreciated. One of the most important ways, however, is by examining the precious and illuminating doctrine of premortal existence. Few truths are so vital for mortals to know in order to increase faith. Few truths push aside so many stumbling blocks and are so personalized in their significance. As we struggle through this otherwise perplexing existence amid the cares and anxieties of the world, the perspective brought by this doctrine is precious and personal indeed.

In a world starved for a sense of human identity and purpose, the light of the restored gospel shines especially brightly through this deep doctrine which tells us of things "in the beginning."

Chapter Three

"A WONDERFUL FLOOD OF LIGHT"

Describing our coming to earth "trailing clouds of glory," as Wordsworth does in his poem "Intimations of Immortality from Recollections of Early Childhood," is certainly evocative imagery. Another writer, though uninstructed by true doctrine, mused insightfully that "everything is arranged in this life as though we entered it carrying the burden of obligations contracted in a former life. . . . obligations which . . . seem to belong to a different world, founded upon kindness . . . which we leave in order to be born into this world" (Marcel Proust, *The Captive*, trans. C. K. Scott Moncrieff [New York: Albert and Charles Boni, 1929], pp. 250–51). Similarly, J. R. R. Tolkien perceptively declared:

Dis-graced [man] may be, yet is not de-throned,
and keeps the rags of lordship once he owned.
(In William Griffin, *Clive Staples Lewis: A Dramatic Life* [San Francisco: Harper and Row, 1986], p. 79.)

However, so much more illuminating than the faint glow of truth emanating from such expressions is the striking brightness of the Restoration's revealed truths. It could not be otherwise, for as Jacob declared, "no man knoweth of [God's] ways save it be revealed unto him" (Jacob 4:8).

The phrase "a wonderful flood of light" is taken from a 1909 First Presidency statement on the origin of man. At that time the First Presidency stated: "The doctrine of the pre-existence, —revealed so plainly, particularly in latter days,—pours a wonderful flood of light upon the otherwise mysterious problem of man's origin" (*Improvement Era*, November 1909, p. 80).

The doctrine of premortality declares that, before his mortal birth, "man was also in the beginning with God" (D&C 93:29). Therefore, as an identifiable individual, you have been you for a long, long time. Furthermore, though some important details are as yet unrevealed, certain spirit elements of man "are eternal" and "have no beginning," since "intelligence, or the light of truth, was not created or made, neither indeed can be." (D&C 93:29, 33.) Joseph Smith added, "it existed from eternity and will exist to eternity" (*Teachings*, p. 158).

Whether as a spirit son or a spirit daughter of our Heavenly Father, each of us was sent here from our first estate to undergo this joyful yet stressful mortal second estate. Being the literal, premortal spirit children of the Father, each of us can, by going from grace to grace, eventually receive of the fulness of the Father, as did Jesus (see D&C 93:20). In addition to being resurrected, we can become "perfect"—or, in one set of meanings from the Greek, "finished," "completed," and "fully developed" —but only if we worship God and truly follow the example of our Redeemer, Jesus Christ. The ultimate adoration is emulation, which helps us to become like those we worship.

As we noted earlier, the Prophet Joseph Smith taught that "if men do not comprehend the character of God, they do not comprehend themselves!" (*Teachings*, p. 343.) However, such comprehending clearly requires an understanding of the doctrine of premortality; we must know that we really are God's spirit children, trailing clouds of glory that contain dimmed flakes of fire still pulsating with the borrowed light from our eternal home!

In some form or degree the vital concept of premortal existence is found in the Bible, in early Christian documents, in Greek and Jewish literature, and in other sources as well. Only from the Restoration, however—the "miraculous miracle," with its confirming and clarifying and its elaborating revelations—do we get the clear and definitive truths about man's origins.

The plain and precious doctrine of premortality, in President Harold B. Lee's words, can provide "an awakened realization of who [we] are" (*Ensign*, January 1974, p. 6). In a similar vein, President Joseph F. Smith said, "Through obedience, we often catch a spark from the awakened memories of the immortal soul, which lights up our whole being as with the glory of our former home" (*Gospel Doctrine* [Salt Lake City: Deseret Book, 1966], p. 14). He further instructed us:

> Notwithstanding this fact that our recollection of former things was taken away, the character of our lives in the spirit world has much to do with our disposition, desires and mentality here in mortal life. This spirit influences the body to a great extent, just as the body in its desires and cravings has an influence on the spirit. . . . Environment and many other causes, however, have great influence on the progress and destiny of man, but we must not lose sight of the fact that the characteristics of the spirit which were developed through many ages of a former existence play a very important part in our progression through mortal life. (*Improvement Era*, March 1916, p. 426.)

In the light of these stimulating concepts, clearly we should think of ourselves not only for what we are but also for what we have the possibility to become!

Prophets in all dispensations have understood these things. Someday, when the obscuring dust of mortal history finally settles, we shall see much more clearly that gospel fulness existed even in Adam's time, including the doctrine of premortality.

In developing and increasing real faith, the doctrine of premortality is a fundamental building block, just as is the doctrine of postmortality. This doctrine of premortality represents a fresh view of ourselves, even a profound response to man's search for meaning in life. It is easy to see how, lacking an understanding of premortality, some find this life puzzling and some regard the human predicament as inexplicable.

Premortality, mortality, and postmortality have been compared to a three-act play, of which we are witnessing the second act. Not having seen (remembered) the first act, we have to rely on reports from those who have received revelation. Those who are without these reports have inadequate knowledge concerning the preceding "there and then," and hence the injustice and unevenness of the "here and now" have caused some to call God's justice into question along with His capacity to achieve His purposes.

Without an understanding of premortality, it is no wonder that mortals often fail to take account of what is perhaps mortality's most prominent feature—its stern proving and tutoring dimensions. Some then use life's trials as an argument against God, instead of accepting these trials as being something "common to man," or as the needed tutorials which, though rigorous, last "but for a small moment" (1 Corinthians 10:13; D&C 122:4).

Mortality is properly designed to permit us only limited vision. Without the perspective of premortality, instead of understanding that "all these things shall give thee experience" (D&C 122:7), we can become drenched in doubt and be wrenched by adversity and irony, lamenting, "Why me? Why this? Why now?"

Without the perspective of a purposeful mortality and also of long-standing, even premortal, covenants, Israel's wanderings make of Sinai a senseless sojourn. However, Israel's wandering is actually a type for our mortal state and God's plans for us: "And thou shalt remember all the way which the Lord thy God led thee these forty years in the wilderness, to humble thee, and to prove thee, to know what was in thine heart, whether thou wouldest keep his commandments, or no" (Deuteronomy 8:2). Just as Israel was proved in the wilderness, God's divine designs for mortality include to "prove [us] herewith" (Abraham 3:25).

Those who are not informed of our pre-earth state are doctrinally deprived mortals and, in Nephi's words, can and will "stumble exceedingly" (1 Nephi 13:34). For instance, a severe stumbling—a major misreading of reality—is evident in the attitude of hopelessness on the part of those who say mankind is "destined to extinction. . . . There is nothing we can do." In one poet's words: "We have no personal life beyond the grave. There is no God. Fate knows nor wrath nor ruth [compassion]." (James Thomson, *The City of Dreadful Night and Other Poems* [London: Bertram Dobell, 1910], p. 35.)

These mortal lamentations bring to mind the great and reassuring lines of Jacob concerning the precious perspective of divine truth: "[The Spirit] . . . speaketh of things as they *really are*, and of things as they *really will be*" (Jacob 4:13, italics added). Truth likewise includes "knowledge of things . . . as they were" (D&C 93:24). Thus truth is the "sum of existence" ("Oh Say, What Is Truth?" *Hymns*, no. 272).

Gaining "life eternal" requires our coming to know "God, and Jesus Christ" (John 17:3). Then, so knowing and so worshipping them, we will genuinely strive to become more like them and seek to partake of their fulness.

For now, however, we mortals merely possess certain underdeveloped possibilities and qualities, qualities such as love, mercy, patience, meekness, and spiritual submissiveness. But though we are enormously less spiritually developed than Jesus, the potential is there, for we too were with the Father "in the beginning."

Many of our religious friends sincerely hold with the tradition that each individual is actually created out of nothing—either at conception or at birth. This is significantly different from knowing that, as differentiated individuals, we were with God "in the beginning" in the premortal world (D&C 93:29).

Thus there is contained in the simple LDS hymn "I Am a Child of God" or in the anthem "O My Father" more true doctrine than in the communiques from various synods and councils of centuries past! Discussion is not a substitute for revelation!

President John Taylor rejoiced that the restored gospel and restored Church helped him "to know . . . by revelation for myself. . . . I want something that is calculated to satisfy the capacious desires of that eternal mind." Otherwise, left uninstructed, said President Taylor "I would worship God the best way I knew how, and act justly and honorably with my neighbor; which I believe thousands of that class of men called infidels do at the present day." (John Taylor, in *Book of Testimonies*, p. 48.)

How and when did this precious doctrine of premortality become lost or distorted? We do not know precisely and completely, even though we recognize that some things were "kept back" and others "taken away" from that which, much later, became our treasured Bible (1 Nephi 13:34, 40). Stephen Robinson of Brigham Young University has written: "One needs to realize that by the time the dispute arose . . . over the origin of souls, the scriptures that answered the question had already been excised, therefore those who deliberated were left to sift through their conflicting traditions without benefit of scripture on this point" (letter to author dated November 29, 1988).

Whatever the particulars, the impact of this "plain and precious" doctrine was stilled for centuries.

It seems that the more spiritually significant the doctrine, the more quickly it comes under attack from the devil, hence the more quickly it is discarded when apostasy occurs. Furthermore, one false doctrine usually leads to another. By way of example, premortality, the reality of a physical resurrection, and the concept that man can become god-like were early casualties in the attack by false doctrines.

Another feature of false doctrines is that almost always they seem to cause a lessened sense of personal identity, of personal accountability, or of personal joy. Mistaken beliefs often lead to a heightened sense of hopelessness about the human circumstance! Thus the doctrinally deprived really do "stumble exceedingly" (1 Nephi 13:34).

Another example of a severe stumbling occurred because of the false doctrine of predestination. Why worship a capricious, unjust God such as this doctrine implies? Before predestination's grip loosened, it helped to set the stage for pervasive irreligion.

Other mutant, secular beliefs postulate their own forms of determinism—economic and historical. Whatever the form, false doctrines diminish human understanding of the reality that we mortals are "free to choose" (2 Nephi 2:27).

Historically, too, a general lack of understanding about God's plan of salvation gave impetus to the ebbing sea of Christian faith, about which Matthew Arnold wrote in his poem "Dover Beach":

> Its melancholy, long, withdrawing roar,
> Retreating, to the breath
> Of the night wind down the vast edges drear
> And naked shingles of the world.

Thus came the Restoration, with this "plain and precious" doctrine, "that faith also might increase in the earth" (D&C 1:21).

Though the absence of vital gospel truths began to be remedied by the Restoration, appreciation and understanding were neither widespread nor immediate among all Church members. Sequentially, though it was not then fully recognized by all, the precious truths concerning premortality were unfolded in accordance with the line-upon-line pattern of revelation. These came first in April or May 1829 (Alma 13), and then with much more clarity and detail in 1830, while Joseph was translating Genesis and received the book of Moses by revelation. More came in 1832 (D&C 76:11-13), in 1833 (D&C 93), and so on. Still more came in 1842 when the book of Abraham was published. Joseph Smith publicly preached a portion of the doctrine of premortality in 1839 (see *Teachings*, p. 158). Later, just prior to his martyrdom, there came the soaring King Follett funeral sermon in April 1844 (see *Teachings*, beginning p. 343).

Most recently, in 1918, we received what is now section 138 of the Doctrine and Covenants.

Whether this gap between early revelation and later articulation reflected imperfect record-keeping, the Lord's timing, Joseph's degree of disclosure (for he did not tell all he knew), the people's readiness to receive, or all of the above, we do not know. In any case, the revelations came incrementally, and Joseph's understanding and articulating apparently came in the same manner.

Presently we may puzzle over those occasions wherein we sense that we belong to another place which is somehow imprinted upon us. In pondering these emotions, we can only speak "the smallest part which [we] feel" (Alma 26:16). There is certainly no sustained surf of recall, but only brief freshening by the delicate mists of memory. These evaporate quickly enough under the baking heat of the mortal day, but only after evoking, however fleetingly, an unmistakable longing in us. Though estranged, we hunger for reunion, for return even though we know not where.

Only a few come to this mortal experience with substantial saintliness already developed. Rather, our individual best is presently but the bud of possibility. Even so, these buds of possibility—the early stages of divine attributes—are unmistakably there. While unfolding and enlarging over time, these key qualities should also "grow together," producing full felicity.

When we experience the celestial qualities in others, even though not fully developed, we rejoice. We rightly associate these traits with greatness—whether in neighbors, friends, or those of high station. The selflessness of Mother Teresa speaks for itself. So did the meekness of that remarkable George Washington.

Since our individual identities and personalities did not begin here in mortality, there emerges a more glorious appreciation of the atonement of Jesus, our Redeemer. As inwardly and reverently we conjoin the scriptures pertaining to the Atonement with the things of the holy temple, the impending real reunion with the Father and real reconciliation to Him have so much greater meaning.

In theological fact, the more complete our understanding of the great atonement, the more it is linked to the premortal world, as Hugh Nibley has so often and so thoughtfully expressed. If, as some mistakenly aver, we had been created here and out of nothing—whether at conception or at birth—how could we, as individuals, really be going home to a place that we, as individuals, never knew? How could there be genuine, individual reconciliation with a Father whom we, as individuals, did not know before our birth?

Actually we were "nurtured" near God's side and then came here for a "wise and glorious purpose" ("O My Father," *Hymns*, no. 292). This all points toward a time when the faithful shall "regain [God's] presence" in resplendent reunion. No wonder Joseph Smith could speak of the "gospel of reconciliation" (*Teachings*, p. 192).

We know almost nothing about ourselves or about conditions before our spirit birth. But whatever existed or whatever we were before that birth, this was incorporated into Father's merciful plans. We became his literal spirit sons and daughters, thereby being ushered into our first estate. Even in the premortal there and then, Father left His children free to choose. Hence the ideological "war in heaven." (See Luke 10:18; JST, Revelation 12:6-8; 2 Nephi 2:17; D&C 29:36.)

During the stressful sojourn on this earth we should make no mistake about who we and others really are. Amid our budding possibilities, in the words of C. S. Lewis, we are "in a society of possible gods and goddesses, . . . [in which] there are no *ordinary* people. [We] have never talked to a mere mortal. Nations, cultures, arts, civilisations—these are mortal, and their life is to ours as the life of a gnat. But it is immortals whom we joke with, work with, marry, snub, and exploit." (C. S. Lewis, *The Weight of Glory and Other Addresses* [New York: Macmillan, 1980], pp. 18-19.)

When we know *who* we are, then we know also much more clearly *what* we might become—and also *how* and *when*. The gospel thereby emancipates us from uncertainty as to our identity. But this precious perspective also brings with it an intensification of our personal accountability, since we know *who* we are and *why* we are here. Actually, several scriptures indicate that the Spirit of the Lord, through conscience, instructs between good and bad all those who will heed it, thereby giving us an accountability which, though we may not appreciate it, is nevertheless there. (See Moroni 7:16–18; 2 Nephi 2:5; John 1:9; D&C 84:46; 88:7; 93:2.)

While "men are, that they might have joy" (2 Nephi 2:25), scriptures repeatedly tell us that the "natural man" clearly prefers perishable pleasure. But with the heightened accountability we have mentioned, how is it, for instance, that an eternal entity, on leave from the royal courts on high, can treat another individual as merely an object of sexual pleasure? Do child abusers realize whose child they have abused? And—at a lower but still significant level of wrongdoing—since Jesus has descended below all things (see D&C 88:6) in order to lift us all up (3 Nephi 27:14), how can we so frequently engage in putting others down?

With regard to poverty and disease, even if people have actually "brought upon [themselves their] misery" (Mosiah 4:17), how can we withhold our assistance, since we know who they really are?

Inasmuch as restored knowledge teaches us we all were "in the beginning" with God and have the potential to be with Him throughout eternity, how childish it is to take advantage of another human—whether in dating, in business, in politics, or in any other area of life! Since God is "lending [us] breath . . . from one moment to another" (Mosiah 2:21), how wrong it is to use any of that precious breath to lie or to bear false witness, or to use that vital energy to "dig a pit for [one's] neighbor"! (2 Nephi 28:8.)

Knowing that we live in eternity, how can we conclude that, because of the fleeting pleasures and pressures of the world, we have no time for children? Furthermore, may not the many wounded strewn along life's way justifiably expect us eternals not to be in too much of a hurry?

Even after all the premortal tutorials, including those for the noble souls "called and prepared from the foundation of the world" (Alma 13:3), we were all placed in a mortal environment amid real challenges that would tame the raw self further. President Lorenzo Snow has suggested that in prospect we may have perceived some of the difficulties we would have to face:

> I dare say that in the spirit world, when it was proposed to us to come into this probation, and pass through the experience that we are now receiving, it was not altogether pleasant and agreeable; the prospects were not so delightful in all respects as might have been desired. Yet there is no doubt that we saw and understood clearly there that, in order to accomplish our exaltation and glory, this was a necessary experience; and however disagreeable it might have appeared to us, we were willing to conform to the will of God, and consequently we are here. (*The Teachings of Lorenzo Snow*, Clyde Williams, comp. [Salt Lake City: Bookcraft, 1984], pp. 92–93.)

"Free to choose" between liberty and life on the one hand and captivity and death on the other (see 2 Nephi 2:27), we now experience firsthand the bitter and the sweet. Even for those souls who were already significantly spiritually submissive, it is a process of polishing. If we are unwilling to participate in the requisite learning experiences, our performance cannot be consecrated for our own good (see 2 Nephi 32:9). Yet "the power is in [us]" to do much good, if we but will (D&C 58:27–28). God's work will truly become our own only as we strive to be more like Him by gaining access to the powers of heaven through increased personal righteousness (see D&C 121:36). But it is no use craving more of God's power without first having more of His love in us. This is what much of our mortal training is all about—coming to an understanding, *through experience*, of how crucial the cardinal, Christian virtues are.

Since we have come into mortality "not in entire forgetfulness," ironical as it may seem our present drives for status, power, and ascendancy may involve twisted, muted memories of glories and dominions we witnessed before we came here. But how can one wisely exercise any extensive dominion without first developing dominion over oneself? We may desire to have spiritual glory and power, but we cannot obtain it without emulating God's qualities and attributes—including humility, a prerequisite to real glory. Moreover, larger, future glory finally involves larger, future service to others. This is obvious in the declared purpose of God's own work and glory (see Moses 1:39). Regal repose and idle indifference clearly are out of place in the celestial kingdom.

During all of our protracted developmental process we are very dependent on God's long-suffering, which provides us with the much-needed time and space in which to repent and to grow (see Alma 12:24; 42:5).

If we fail to learn who we are, however much other information we acquire here, we shall be "ever learning, and never able to come to the knowledge of the truth" (2 Timothy 3:7). Without the key spiritual truths, such as premortality, learning will be a Sisyphus-like process in which

> All ignorance toboggans into know
> and trudges up to ignorance again.
> (Edward Estlin Cummings, "One Times One.")

With the acceptance of knowledge about premortality comes a greater realization of what it means to be true to ourselves and to our possibilities. We can even understand better the role of life's disappointments and of opposition, the full shock of which we will still feel, despite that understanding, but now within the absorptive framework of faith.

Having that knowledge, no longer can we regard other people as mere ciphers, functions, or even as temporary friends — because in spiritual fact they were, are, and will continue to be our eternal brothers and sisters. One first weeps for joy because of such stunning perspectives, and weeps next because of *what is* among mortals as compared to *what should be*.

Does such doctrinal knowledge automatically produce love for others? No. But the doctrines create a climate in which the development of sustained love is possible. We have added reasons to try to love. We have reasons to endure any lack of love for us by mortals, knowing who it is that loves us perfectly. We have reasons to think of ourselves not only for what we are but also for what we have the possibilities to become.

Having the true doctrines, not only are we made aware of many more things in our lives which need to be put right but also there are now powerful and persuasive reasons to put them right!

By the light of the Restoration we see that, with us, other mortals are members of an eternal community. Our obligations and ethics in that community transcend those that are merely mutually agreed upon for the moment. One devastating weakness of "situational" ethics is their provincial failure to take into account man's real and full situation—his eternal history and possibilities.

When illuminated by true doctrine, it is no wonder that life's process must be so relentless! There is so much to be done in so little time. Thus a blessing is often quickly succeeded by a soul-stretching. Spiritual exhilaration is soon followed by frustration or temptation. Reveries are followed by adversities, since, left too long in extended spiritual musings, we would quickly forget others in need. We must get on with the next challenge.

Blessed with our knowledge of premortal experience, life is largely what we choose to make of it and of our inborn talents. The same musical scale was available to Beethoven for composing his Fifth Symphony as to the composer of "Chopsticks." These compositions even share several opening notes of melody. But what an enormous difference in substance and effect!

So here we are in Eden, an Eden become Babylon! Perhaps we have grown too accustomed to the place. Even if we decide to leave Babylon, some of us endeavor to keep a second residence there, or we commute on weekends. To quote President Marion G. Romney, some go on "trying to serve the Lord without offending the devil" ("The Price of Peace," in *Speeches of the Year* [Provo: Brigham Young University, March 1, 1955], p. 7).

Furthermore, Babylon does not give exit permits gladly—an ironic implementation of that ancient boast, "one soul shall not be lost" (Moses 4:1). Babylon is also a noisy, distracting place. No wonder some therein are "called many times and . . . would not hear" (Alma 10:6). No wonder Jesus' open invitation to leave Babylon's slums and to join Him in the stunning, spiritual highlands goes largely unheeded. There, however, redeeming Jesus waits "with open arms to receive [us]" (Mormon 6:17).

With an understanding of the fulness of the gospel that embraces the remote past, we can see our lives here as part of a continuum rather than being deceived by the philosophy of "eat, drink, and be merry, for tomorrow we die" (2 Nephi 28:7). Gospel fulness likewise replaces the algebra of agnosticism with its one "known" factor, all others being unknown; the Restoration also refutes humanism's statement quoted in chapter 1: "No deity will save us; we must save ourselves."

Eliza R. Snow lyricized about our yearnings for the heavenly home we left and for our return to it, saying that it was not "until the key of knowledge was restored" that she knew "why" ("O My Father," *Hymns*, no. 292). That key of knowledge is "the fulness of [the Lord's] scriptures" (JST, Luke 11:53). The religious establishment of Jesus' time not only twisted what scriptures they had but they also lacked "the key of knowledge," the "plain and precious things" (Luke 11:52; 1 Nephi 13:40).

The very preciousness of the Restoration, with its knowledge of eternal principles and foreordained assignments, makes it unwise for us to tamper with its truths, to attempt to dilute its doctrines, or to misuse its authority. Why in any case would one want to belong to a church which he could remake in his own image? Rather, it is the Lord's image we should come to have in our countenances (see Alma 5:19). The doctrines are His—not ours. The power is His to delegate, not ours to manipulate. Those who want to shape and remake things to their own liking have ample and legitimate opportunities to do so in political parties and mortal organizations. Our spiritual task, however, as previously commissioned, is to make God's work our own, not the other way around.

There are also those in this second estate, whether consciously or otherwise, who try running away from God. Running away from God, no less! God who has created worlds without number and yet notices the fall of every sparrow! Such runaways cannot even make it unnoticed off the porch, let alone into the suburbs.

Besides, returning prodigals—those who have been all over the world and even some parts of their hometown—soberly but gladly confirm that it is impossible to run away from God's love or beyond His redemptive reach. How He persists, for His "arm is lengthened out all the day long"! (2 Nephi 28:32.)

What we know of the premortal past indicates that God's love for us is of even greater duration than we can comprehend. Should we not suppose, given any ancient or inherent individuality on our part and given our opportunity to choose, that our Father is doing with us the best that even He can do? The marvel is that He persists and pursues His plan of happiness for us while preserving our freedom to choose! God is truly an organizing as well as a loving Father. Back of the beyond He saw what was, but He also saw what could be! Recognizing the great distance we had to travel from where we were, seeing our flaws, and nevertheless being willing to commence His work with whatever was before our spirit birth, God loved us enough to initiate and sustain this divine process over measureless periods. There appears to have been "no other way" for Him to increase our happiness and our joy. What long-suffering love! What true fatherhood!

As He made clear to us back in those premortal times, all of God's works are designed so that we might be "added upon," thereby enjoying greater happiness and pointing to the eventual day, when, if faithful, we might partake of all that the Father has (see D&C 84:38).

Indeed we should daily stand even more amazed at the love God proffers us. As we learned when His plan was unfolded to us in heaven, He was willing to allow the sacrifice of his first-born spirit Son, His Only Begotten in the flesh, in order to be the example for us and to redeem us. As unfathomable as are our Father's intelligence and power, even more staggering is the felicitous fact of His eternal, perfect love. Even as we come to love Him, as the Apostle reminded us, God loved us first (see 1 John 4:19).

For our own benefit God wants things to "be done in [His] own way" (D&C 104:16). Yet all the while, He endures our ingratitude, our insensitivity, and our relapses. All the while, too, He honors our individuality.

When our premortal memories are restored, this will give us even more reasons to praise God forever! When judgment day arrives and all mortals kneel and confess before Him, each will openly acknowledge that God's love, His justice, and His mercy are perfect (see Alma 12:15). In my opinion, this grateful acknowledgment will pertain not only to this second estate but to all of our remarkable relationship with Him! He does nothing save it be for our benefit (see 2 Nephi 26:24).

"Oh, it is wonderful!" the hymn says ("I Stand All Amazed," *Hymns*, no. 193). God was redemptively at work long before mortal time began on this earth—and He will still be at work even after mortal time is no more (see D&C 88:110; Alma 40:8).

The Restoration enlarges our collective memory (see Alma 37:8) beyond present imagination, through the coming forth of more scripture—along with the promise of much, much more to come. The doctrine of premortality is among what Paul called "the deep things of God," which God has revealed to us afresh in the latter days (1 Corinthians 2:10; Jacob 4:8, 13). For that divinely dispatched "wonderful flood of light" which illuminates this deep doctrine and by which we can see "things as they really are" let us "live in thanksgiving daily" (Alma 34:38).

Chapter Four

"O Remember, Remember" . . . "Murmur Not"

Remembering and counting our many blessings can humble us by reminding us of all the reasons we have to be thankful to God—not just today's reasons, but those relating to all our yesterdays. Each week a sincere partaking of the sacrament can become part of this very process. We partake "in remembrance," so that we may "always remember" what Jesus has done for us (3 Nephi 18:11; Moroni 4, 5).

If we fail to stir remembrance of blessings received, the human tendency is to say, in effect, whether to one's God or to one's fellows, "What have you done for me lately?" Indeed, prophets of the Lord have asked directly whether their people had "sufficiently retained in remembrance" His deliverances and blessings (Alma 5:6–7). It is best to cultivate our "remembering" capacity now and to be guided accordingly, since at judgment day we will have "perfect remembrance" (Alma 5:18).

The important theme of remembrance occurs in one form or another in the Old Testament well over two hundred times. It appears in the Book of Mormon dozens of times, too. This parallelism is to be expected, since the Israelites in Palestine observed the law of Moses and the Nephites kept it "strictly" for many years (see Mosiah 13:30; Alma 30:3). Wherever the gospel is, there too is the call to remembrance.

If we are not living "in thanksgiving daily" (Alma 34:38), remembering "sufficiently" sometimes requires severe stimulation: "And thus we see that except the Lord doth chasten his people with many afflictions, yea, except he doth visit them with death and with terror, and with famine and with all manner of pestilence, they will not remember him" (Helaman 12:3).

It is much better to be humble "because of the word" and because of our many blessings (Alma 32:14). Without such meekness, we may let a present deprivation or affliction blot out our remembrance of past blessings. Even the very best people sometimes receive stern reminders: "Thou art not yet as Job" (D&C 121:10). "The Son of Man hath descended below them all. Art thou greater than he?" (D&C 122:8.) The impressive brother of Jared was chastened because for a season he had been forgetful of his prayers (see Ether 2:14).

The sheer weight of our cumulative reasons to be grateful can help us to live in thanksgiving daily. If so disposed, we can feel sufficiently grateful to "sing the song of redeeming love" about both now and days past! (Alma 5:26; 34:38.) Not only have we "proved him in days that are past" but also we have been proven, which should encourage us amid present challenges.

The Lord's blessings are of differing kinds, of course, a fact of which we should be conscious as we tally and inventory. Each and every blessing is to be remembered. But the Lord wants us to remember certain blessings most of all.

For instance, Jesus miraculously provided loaves and fishes for the hungry multitude of several thousand (see John 6:1–14). Within minutes the loaves and fishes (of which there were "enough and to spare") were gone. The next morning some of the beneficiaries of that remarkable blessing were hungry again.

Jesus Himself observed, "Your fathers did eat [the miraculous] manna in the wilderness, and are dead." They would have remained forever dead, too, except for the blessing of the Atonement, a blessing which in its effects is infinite and endless, not temporary. In contrast to the daily-dissolving manna, Jesus is the "true bread from heaven," filling us forever so that we will "never hunger." (See John 6:31–58.)

Even so, we rightly pray for our daily bread. It would be much more difficult to read the scriptures if we were hungry, or to serve neighbors if we ourselves were starving. Having supplied the daily bread, then, the Lord generously provides us with the nourishment of the holy scriptures upon which we are invited to feast daily (see 2 Nephi 31:20; John 5:39). If we fail to attend the feast, if we do not search the scriptures, we will miss the needed and reminding truths that God has sent among us for that purpose. That would be analogous to the situation that produced Jesus' heartfelt lamentation, "Oh, Jerusalem, Jerusalem, how oft . . . ," demonstrating that His contemporaries did not recognize who had come among them.

Those of us in the United States are rightly concerned with preserving our precious constitutional liberties, including freedom of religion, speech, and press. Events in the world often remind us of our need for thanksgiving over the liberties we enjoy. Throughout history most mortals have not had any such constitutional liberties, yet they were still blessed in other ways. For instance, mortal property rights have often been either non-existent, revoked, or easily lost, but this is not so with regard to a partly earned, partly grace-provided title to one of the many mansions in Heavenly Father's abode.

At night, two millennia ago, the celebration of the great Feast of Tabernacles featured illuminated candelabra in the courtyard of the temple at Jerusalem. Fresh from that experience the Master Teacher went on to declare that He was the Light of the world, that His followers, regardless of time or season, need never walk in darkness (see John 8:12).

In this age we are blessed daily by electrical light. It takes a power failure to remind us how much we take that blessing for granted. As Jesus told his followers in the above passage, however, there is never a spiritual power failure when the gospel "casts away the veil of unbelief" and dispels "the cloud of darkness," thus producing an endless daytime of understanding and rejoicing. The gospel can "light up [our] minds," so that we can function as illuminated individuals — without interruption. (See Alma 19:6.)

As we continue to remember our blessings, we note that we can, and in fact do, receive wonderful blessings which end searing pain or which extend our lives productively. How deeply and justifiably grateful we are for such blessings! More important, however, we need to remember that the Lord gives us transcendent immortality — unconditionally! Additionally, He offers us the abundance of eternal life. If we keep our covenants, a million years from now it will not matter in one sense whether we died in 1990, 1993, or 2010. How we live in any seemingly "extra" years does matter, of course, insofar as our use of time bears upon our qualifying for eternal life and assists others in that same process. And it is worth remembering that covenant keepers perform similar duties and services on either side of the veil of death, since the second estate continues until the resurrection.

There are important gradations as between types of blessings. One type — very real and much appreciated — is tied to temporal conditions. We might call these operational revelations — how to build an ark, or how to illuminate barges, for example. These are remarkable blessings which respond to urgent needs, but they cannot compare to the illuminating revelations from Jesus concerning what we must do to be more like Him. That type of blessing is tied to the eternal conditions. Both types are needed. Both are to be remembered.

No wonder the Lord reminded ancient Israel so many times of the need to remember both types of blessings. He often rehearsed their need to remember how they had been rescued so dramatically from Egypt. They even sang a special song to celebrate the miraculous parting and hovering of the Red Sea (see Exodus 15). But it is so much more important that all humans, including ancient Israel, have been rescued from enveloping, endless death. There will be no extinction and no annihilation, and that is precisely because of the marvelous "infinite atonement" (2 Nephi 9:7; Alma 34:10).

Our own memories are not the only things available to us. One purpose of holy scripture is, in fact, to "enlarge" our perspectives and our collective memory (Alma 37:8). It gives us an enhanced "recall." The title page to the Book of Mormon even indicates that the book was written partly "to show unto the remnant of the House of Israel what great things the Lord hath done for their fathers." From the title page on throughout the book, and even in the very close of the Book of Mormon, the theme of remembrance is apparent: "Behold, I would exhort you that when ye shall read these things, if it be wisdom in God that ye should read them, that ye would remember how merciful the Lord hath been unto the children of men, from the creation of Adam even down until the time that ye shall receive these things, and ponder it in your hearts" (Moroni 10:3).

Forgetfulness can be so very expensive: "And also all that generation were gathered unto their fathers: and there arose another generation after them, which knew not the Lord, nor yet the works which he had done for Israel" (Judges 2:10).

How far back should our memories be rolled back? As a beginning, certainly the rollback should cover the length of our personal lives. It requires energy and intellectual honesty to make such an introspective inventory and to keep it before us. Amulek reflected honestly, correcting an initial perception with remembrance:

> And behold, I am also a man of no small reputation among all those who know me; yea, and behold, I have many kindreds and friends, and I have also acquired much riches by the hand of my industry.
>
> Nevertheless, after all this, I never have known much of the ways of the Lord, and his mysteries and marvelous power. I said I never had known much of these things; but behold, I mistake, for I have seen much of his mysteries and his marvelous power; yea, even in the preservation of the lives of this people.

Nevertheless, I did harden my heart, for I was called many times and I would not hear; therefore I knew concerning these things, yet I would not know; therefore I went on rebelling against God, in the wickedness of my heart. (Alma 10:4-6.)

We should likewise journey as far back as the light of scriptures can inform us concerning our collective "memory." The human family has been much blessed from Adam on down:

And thus the Gospel began to be preached, from the beginning, being declared by holy angels sent forth from the presence of God, and by his own voice, and by the gift of the Holy Ghost.

And thus all things were confirmed unto Adam, by an holy ordinance, and the Gospel preached, and a decree sent forth, that it should be in the world, until the end thereof; and thus it was. (Moses 5:58-59.)

And they began from that time forth to call on his name; therefore God conversed with men, and made known unto them the plan of redemption, which had been prepared from the foundation of the world; and this he made known unto them according to their faith and repentance and their holy works (Alma 12:30).

No wonder the Lord asks us to extend our remembrance all the way back:

Remember the days of old, consider the years of many generations: ask thy father, and he will shew thee; thy elders, and they will tell thee.

When the most High divided to the nations their inheritance, when he separated the sons of Adam, he set the bounds of the people according to the number of the children of Israel. (Deuteronomy 32:7-8.)

Yet there have been still other blessings from God, blessings bestowed even longer ago. The Prophet Joseph declared of an ancient scene that brought forth subsequent divine bestowals:

The great Jehovah contemplated the whole of the events connected with the earth, pertaining to the plan of salvation, before it rolled into existence, or ever "the morning stars sang together" for joy; the past, the present, and the future were and are, with Him, one eternal "now;" He knew of . . . the depth of iniquity that would be connected with the human family, . . . and has made ample provision for their redemption (*Teachings*, p. 220).

How thankful we should be that God is not only a loving God but also a God of marvelous capacity who has declared, "I am able to do mine own work" (2 Nephi 27:20, 21). What a great reassurance this is to us, for there are many mortals who acknowledge God but nevertheless doubt that His purposes for humankind will prevail.

Each individual is also blessed with the "light of Christ" (John 1:9; D&C 84:46). One function of this light is to help us to remember—if we do not live so as to dim that light.

When we get our premortal memories back, these will give us further cause to be even more grateful to God—deepening in us the spirit of a perpetual Thanksgiving; for then we will acknowledge that God's justice and mercy have been perfect throughout the total span of our remarkable relationship with Him (see Mosiah 16:1; Alma 12:15). While for the moment we cannot recall our first estate, we can anticipate our third estate and its promised blessings.

We were with God "in the beginning," and all His works have been done so that we might be "added upon" and might have greater happiness—pointing to the eventual day when, if faithful, we might partake of His fulness, even, as Jesus has said, "all that my Father hath" (D&C 84:38, 93:19). This is eternal life, the greatest of all God's gifts (see D&C 14:7), and we should be most thankful for it.

God's love, patience, and long-suffering saw us through our first estate and will do likewise now, through our second estate, as part of His work "to bring to pass the immortality and eternal life of man" (Moses 1:39).

Eternal life is so much more than endless existence. Its fulness, presently inconceivable to us, will involve music and scenery and perspectives which have not "entered into the heart of man" (1 Corinthians 2:9), things we "never had supposed" (Moses 1:10). This blessing will come in the Malachi Measure—so much "that there shall not be room enough to receive it" (Malachi 3:10). Cups running over and without ceasing! Included will be the inestimable and crowning blessings of living in God's presence and of eternal increase!

Upon receiving eternal life, whatever the deprivations of the faithful will have been in mortality, fulness will follow. Mortal deprivations will give way to God's celestial benefactions. And He does not give grudgingly. Being a perfect Father, He delights to honor those who serve Him (see D&C 76:5).

What sort of individuals will receive eternal life? Among others, the few rich who sought the kingdom first and wanted riches only in order to do good (see Jacob 2:18–19); those few who learned not to cease hearkening to the counsels of God (see 2 Nephi 9:29); those few whose hearts were not set upon the praise and things of this world; those few who did not abuse power and authority; the few who learned to obtain and handle the very powers of heaven through significant personal righteousness (see D&C 121:35, 36, 39).

Missing from that glorious scene will be those who remained too concerned with keeping their places in the society's establishments and with receiving the honors and praise of men; those who neglected the poor and needy; those who gained the world but lost their souls in the process; those who could not stop murmuring; those who were not valiant in their testimony of Jesus. (See John 12:42–43; D&C 104:17–18; Matthew 16:26; D&C 76:79.)

Mercifully, things then will "be done in [God's] own way," not ours (D&C 104:16). Then God's purposes, His patience, His power, and His profound love, which were at work long before time was, will also be at work even after time will be no more (see D&C 84:100; Alma 40:8).

These and other truths are among what Paul called "the deep things of God" (1 Corinthians 2:10), for which we should be deeply grateful. Deep truths are for remembering especially when we are in deep difficulty. Even so, "no chastening for the present seemeth to be joyous, but grievous: nevertheless afterward it yieldeth the peaceable fruit of righteousness unto them which are exercised thereby" (Hebrews 12:11). Meanwhile such calisthenics—spiritual equivalents of push-ups and deep knee bends—will still hurt and sorely stretch us. With our gospel knowledge, however, we can understand what the vexing, unceasing "drill" is all about and will recognize that such basic training will not go on forever.

No wonder we have abundant causes to live "in thanksgiving daily" (Alma 34:38)—for all that we have received in the first estate, for all we have received in the second estate, and also in anticipation of the great blessings which we shall receive in our third and final estate!

For now, we pray for various blessings, sometimes for nothing more than a needed night's sleep, or importuningly and justifiably for a grandchild's greater happiness, or for a friend to be healed, or to be better able to endure present affliction. When we receive such blessings—"Praise be to God!" But transcending all such praise should be our everlasting praise to God for His plan of happiness—for making us the very center of His work and purposes! (See 2 Nephi 26:24.)

Meanwhile, too, we are to "take up the cross daily" (Luke 9:23), and again, we will carry it better if we also "live in thanksgiving daily." Granted, even a strong sense of past blessings cannot completely rout present pain or loneliness. After all, we are here to experience (see Genesis 30:27; D&C 122:7). However, memories can become the vigilant sentries needed to challenge our marauding moods, moods which otherwise would carry the day and especially the night! Those sentries can both prod us and point us to the strait and narrow path.

Wise King Benjamin urged us to consider "the blessed and happy state of those that keep the commandments of God," for they will "dwell with God in a state of never-ending happiness. O remember, remember that these things are true." (Mosiah 2:41.)

God never forgets us, even those who turn away from or deny Him. If they repent and come unto Him, He will be merciful to them, "for [His] arm is lengthened out all the day long" (2 Nephi 28:32).

The directness and specificity Jesus employed with the rich and righteous young man who "went away grieved" (Mark 10:22) provided the man with the basis of later remembrance. Could there have been some second thoughts? We do not know whether the good young man subsequently changed his mind after having gone away sorrowing. But Jesus' instructions were pointed enough to make such poignant remembering possible.

We do know that there were those in the religious establishment in the time of Jesus' mortal messiahship who believed on Him in secret but who would not confess Him publicly (John 12:42–43). Later on, after His crucifixion, "a great company" of priests joined the Church, and perhaps among that company were some who earlier had been reluctant to go public and now remembered Jesus (see Acts 6:7).

Without remembrance, the tendency, individual and collective, is to be selfish:

> Yet did not the chief butler remember Joseph, but forgat him (Genesis 40:23).

> Only take heed to thyself, and keep thy soul diligently, lest thou forget the things which thine eyes have seen, and lest they depart from thy heart all the days of thy life: but teach them thy sons, and thy sons' sons (Deuteronomy 4:9).

> Yea, and we may see at the very time when he doth prosper his people, yea, in the increase of their fields, their flocks and their herds, and in gold, and in silver, and in all manner of precious things of every kind and art; sparing their lives, and delivering them out of the hands of their enemies; softening the hearts of their enemies that they should not declare wars against them; yea, and in fine, doing all things for the

welfare and happiness of his people; yea, then is the time that they do harden their hearts, and do forget the Lord their God, and do trample under their feet the Holy One—yea, and this because of their ease, and their exceedingly great prosperity (Helaman 12:2).

While all of the five senses feed memory, they are not memory itself. This is one reason why we must deliberately cultivate memory, especially of the things that matter most.

Another great blessing flowing from remembering is that without remembrance of past blessings we are much more likely to murmur. Murmuring is sometimes defined as a half-supressed or muttered complaint, like Tevye's frequent verbal asides to God in *Fiddler on the Roof.*

Today's crowding concerns bump aside thoughts of yesterday's blessings. Being so alert to the needs of "now" tends to dull us as to yesterday. Moreover, if we do not ponder the past, the future also comes to mean less and less. A worse possibility is that what little remembering some do may involve only the nurturing of an ancient grievance rather than the remembering of a lesson learned. And often that leads to murmuring.

Murmuring crosses the scriptural spectrum of complaints: "We need bread and water" (Numbers 21:5); "The needed provisions and military reinforcements have not arrived" (Alma 60); "Why did we ever leave Egypt?" (Numbers 11:20); "Why did we ever leave Jerusalem?" (1 Nephi 2:11.) Some have murmured, perhaps understandably, over such things as persecution by unbelievers and even over what the name of Christ's Church should be (see Mosiah 27:1; 3 Nephi 27:4). It is ironical that even receiving more scripture from God would cause murmuring (see 2 Nephi 29:8).

An early scriptural instance of murmuring involved Cain's offering to the Lord (see Moses 5:20–21). Though ancient, this episode remains instructively intact, advising us that our motivations and intentions are at least as important as our outward deeds. Cain was "wroth" that Abel's offering was acceptable but his was not. Sometimes we too worry if someone else seems more favored of the Lord than we; worse still, we want to be accepted of the Lord—but on our terms!

The real "addressee" of some murmuring is clearly the Lord. The people who complained against Moses were actually "murmuring against the Lord" (see Exodus 16:8; see also 1 Nephi 16:20). At least Tevye honestly acknowledged whom he addressed in his asides.

Jude tells us something about the style, substance, and motives of some murmurers: "These are murmurers, complainers, walking after their own lusts; and their mouth speaketh great swelling words, having men's persons in admiration because of advantage" (Jude 1:16).

In its extremity, murmuring issues not only from the very discontented but also from the very conflicted: "And they did not come unto Jesus with broken hearts and contrite spirits, but they did curse God, and wish to die. Nevertheless they would struggle with the sword for their lives." (Mormon 2:14.)

Some people murmured against Jesus because He declared Himself to be the Bread of life, saying: "Is not this Jesus, the son of Joseph, whose father and mother we know? how is it then that he saith, I came down from heaven? Jesus therefore answered and said unto them, Murmur not among yourselves." (John 6:42–43.)

Murmuring took place also when Jesus befriended and dined with publicans and sinners, and likewise when a devout woman used expensive ointment to anoint Him (see Luke 5:30; Mark 14:3–9).

In His parable of the workers in the vineyard, Jesus noted of devoted Church members that those who had worked from the first hour, having "borne the burden and the heat of the day," murmured because they received the same wages as those who had worked only the last hour (see Matthew 20:11). We are so concerned with our entitlements—an odd response for beggars to make (see Mosiah 4:19–20).

Laman and Lemuel murmured against father Lehi for leading them into the wilderness because of the "foolish imaginations of his heart" (1 Nephi 2:11). Laman and Lemuel also murmured because they feared going up against powerful and prestigious Laban (see 1 Nephi 3:31; 4:4). In fact, that depressing duo declared that father Lehi had judged the Jerusalemites too harshly—this even though their wickedness was such that Jerusalem was soon to fall and its people would be taken away into bondage! Sometimes, like Laman and Lemuel, we are too provincial and fail to understand "the dealings" of God. (1 Nephi 2:12; 17:22.)

Lehi rebuked the murmuring Laman and Lemuel because of their complaint that Nephi had said "hard things" against them (1 Nephi 16:3). Father Lehi later observed, "That which ye call anger was the truth" (2 Nephi 1:26). How often we can make that same mistake! Cutting truth can surely hurt, but the compensation is that its painful lancing can drain off pride.

There was more murmuring from Laman and Lemuel because Nephi broke his steel bow, because he supposedly couldn't build a ship, and because as the younger brother he was seen as trying to "rule over us" (see 1 Nephi 16:18; 17:17; 2 Nephi 5:3). These same murmurers, however, soon surfeited themselves on the meat brought back from Nephi's hunts with his new bow, and they were glad enough to sail in the ship Nephi built. How handy good but imperfect leaders are as focal points for our frustrations! Especially if they must hold their tongues and simply take it! We have all heard it: "Why don't the Brethren . . . ?"

Nephi is described as being favored of the Lord because he did not murmur (1 Nephi 3:6). So far as we know, he never yielded to grumbling.

In modern times, Oliver Cowdery fell short of the coveted privilege of translating. The Lord told him, "Do not murmur, my son, for it is wisdom in me that I have dealt with you after this manner" (D&C 9:6). Emma Smith was likewise told to "murmur not" because in the divine wisdom certain things were withheld from her (D&C 25:4).

Murmuring can block the process of needed tutoring. Yet unappreciated tutoring surely causes murmuring. It is as if we have an unrealistic expectation that life is to flow smoothly, featuring an unbroken corridor of green lights leading to vacant parking places just in front of our destinations!

As we ponder the foregoing and other examples from scripture, additional points become obvious.

First, the murmurer often lacks the courage to express openly his or her concern. If the complaint concerns a peer, the murmurer usually does not follow this counsel from Jesus: "Moreover if thy brother shall trespass against thee, go and tell him his fault between thee and him alone: if he shall hear thee, thou hast gained thy brother" (Matthew 18:15).

Second, murmurers make good conversational cloak-holders (see Acts 7:58). Though picking up no stones themselves, they provoke others to do so.

Third, while a murmurer insists on venting his own feelings, he regards any response to them as hostile (see 2 Nephi 1:26). For example, murmurers apparently do not usually take into account the bearing capacity of the receivers.

Fourth, murmurers usually are short on memory. The Israelites survived in Sinai. They were sometimes hungry and thirsty, but the Lord always rescued them, whether by quail or by water struck from a rock (see Numbers 11:31; Exodus 17:6). With no remembering of past blessings, however, there is no perspective available for evaluating present dissatisfactions. Perspective about what is really going on can be precious indeed: "And thou shalt remember all the way which the Lord thy God led thee these forty years in the wilderness, to humble thee, and to prove thee, to know what was in thine heart, whether thou wouldest keep his commandments, or no" (Deuteronomy 8:2).

It is strange how those short on memory often have long lists of demands.

Perhaps the most fundamental thing to be said about murmuring, however, is contained in this verse: "And thus Laman and Lemuel. . . . did murmur because they knew not the dealings of that God who had created them." (1 Nephi 2:12.)

Having necessarily been out of contact with Pahoran for some time, Moroni complained to him by letter about the government's neglect of the armies, but it turned out that he did not have all the facts. Pahoran's response is a classic in meekness and empathy! (See Alma 60–61.) The story shows that people can be out of touch not only with the facts but also with each other. Murmuring frequently comes about when the murmurer has insufficient information to make a correct judgment; and this emphasizes that having confidence in leaders who keep confidences is part of sustaining them.

For us, as laborers in the Lord's vineyard, to murmur over life's inequities is, Jesus indicated, "to murmur against the good-man of the house" (Matthew 20:11). The goodness of the Lord of the house is attested to in many ways, yet as guests many of us still murmur about present accommodations.

Whether it concerns the impending fall of Jerusalem or the tutoring of Oliver Cowdery, murmuring questions God's capacity. Yet He has assured us, "I am able to do mine own work" (2 Nephi 27:20, 21). Furthermore, He has even told us that certain experiences, over which we might otherwise murmur, can actually be for our good (see D&C 122:7; see also Genesis 30:27; D&C 105:10).

As in the case of the episode of the golden calf, the view from the desert floor is very different from that atop Mount Sinai. Perspective makes such an enormous difference. Let us not forget that, aside from the extent of its disclosure before he was cast out of heaven, Satan does not know the mind of God (see Moses 4:6).

Privy to the Father's thoughts because of His humility, Jesus, on the other hand, knew so much more; in fact, "he needed not that any man should teach him" (JST, Matthew 3:24–25).

As if damage to self were not enough reason to resist murmuring, another obvious danger is its contagiousness. Such was the case even with faithful father Lehi, who, for one brief moment, got caught up in the contagion of murmuring (see 1 Nephi 16:20). When Moses once lapsed briefly, it was under exasperating circumstances that included pressure from rebels (see Numbers 20:7–12). No one knows how to work a crowd better than the adversary.

Elders Brigham Young and Heber C. Kimball tried to discourage Thomas B. Marsh's murmuring, but to no avail. Later, Brother Marsh said in humble self-disclosure:

> I must have lost the Spirit of the Lord out of my heart. . . .
> I became jealous of the Prophet . . . and overlooked everything that was right, and spent all my time in looking for the evil; . . . I thought I saw a beam in Brother Joseph's eye, but it was nothing but a mote, and my own eye was filled with the beam; . . . as Brother Heber C. Kimball says, I got mad and I wanted everybody else to be mad. I talked with Brother Brigham Young and Brother Heber C. Kimball, and I wanted them to be mad like myself; and I saw they were not mad, and I got madder still because they were not. Brother Brigham Young, with a cautious look, said, "Are you the leader of the Church, Brother Thomas?" I answered "No." "Well then," said he, "why do you not let that alone?" (Thomas B. Marsh, *Book of Testimonies*, pp. 103, 105.)

Often those who murmur do it sarcastically. Sarcasm can not only prove contagious but also can provide a clever verbal rallying point for the otherwise unfocused and unexpressed feelings. Yet our responsibilities to each other involve more than merely reporting or otherwise displaying how we feel. Being of good cheer itself can be contagious, and it is certainly more in accord with our obligation to strengthen each other and to do things "with cheerful hearts and countenances" (D&C 81:5; 59:15).

Two of the basic things over which we are to be justifiably of good cheer are the transcendent blessings that our sins are forgiven and that Jesus has overcome the world. Additionally, we are assured that He is in our midst, He will lead us along, and He will stand by us. (See John 16:33; Matthew 9:2; D&C 61:36; 88:6; 78:18.) Therefore, knowing that these major and everlasting things are in place, we can better endure such mundane trials as a frustrating traffic jam. And at those times we can be calm enough to ask ourselves how it can rain on the just and the unjust alike (Matthew 5:45) without occasionally raining on our parade.

Even while in deep difficulties, those of deep faith are generously disposed, as was reflected in Helaman's report to Moroni from the battle front: "Behold, we do not know but what ye are unsuccessful, . . . if so, we do not desire to murmur. . . . But behold, it mattereth not—we trust God will deliver us, notwithstanding the weakness of our armies, yea, and deliver us out of the hands of our enemies." (Alma 58:35, 37.)

The phrase "it mattereth not" bespeaks a faithful people, filled with precious perspective, who are reluctant to murmur. Job too was like that. He endured much adversity but was anxious that he not "charge God foolishly" (Job 1:22).

Of course there are ways—both formal and informal—by which properly to express legitimate concerns, and even complaints, productively (see Matthew 18:15). These will go unused, however, if one's real desire is to let off scalding steam; there is, of course, so much more heat than light in steam. Yes, we can gripe or grumble merely in a passing way, even cleverly and self-effacingly, reflecting a passing irritation. But even mild murmuring can be more pointed and directed than we might care to admit.

Murmuring can be another form of mocking God's plan of salvation, like filing a minority report suggesting that what God has planned is not fully adequate (3 Nephi 29:6). Yes, God has an overall plan, but we don't care for His specific timing—perhaps because he has not advised us as to the detail (see Enos 1:16; Ether 3:24, 27; 2 Nephi 27:21). Yet we are specifically advised that "all things must come to pass in their time" (D&C 64:32).

Yes, we may acknowledge His overall plan but criticize His style, because He does things in His own way (Jacob 4:8; D&C 1:16; 56:14). We would prefer that things be done in our way, even though our ways are much lower than His (see Isaiah 55:8–9). The different, lower perceptions on Sinai's desert floor resulted in the golden calf, a contrast for which there are obvious analogies today.

We might add that God has told us He intends to try our faith and our patience (see Mosiah 23:21). Such stress is the setting from which murmuring most often emerges.

God's timing, which calls for our patience, is often His way of preserving our agency. We halt at a busy intersection when we hear sirens; we pull over for fire trucks. Spiritual emergencies are no different, except that, alas, there are no loud sirens to be heard!

God's long-suffering is sometimes necessary to provide additional opportunities for us to repent. We may think God is merely marking time when actually He is marking openings for us which are sorely needed. But despite this patient care, we are slow to escape from the familiar cell of selfishness.

Perhaps when we murmur we are unconsciously complaining over not being able to cut a special deal with the Lord—we want full blessings but without giving full obedience to the laws upon which those blessings are predicated.

Murmuring can prevent a person from realizing it is time to quit soaking himself in the hot tub of self-pity! Each of us might ask himself how many times he or she has ended up having rich experiences but only after having resisted them at first, sometimes while griping and kicking before reaching the tremendous view that lay just over the next ridge.

Murmuring over the weight of one's cross not only takes energy otherwise needed to carry it but also might cause another to put his cross down altogether.

The load we feel doesn't come solely from our gripes; mostly it comes from the weight of our unkept promises and our unresolved sins. These press down heavily upon us, and while murmuring relieves us through temporary catharsis, it also deflects us from facing what needs to be done. Thus in his surrender to God, the true believer says, with the Lamanite king, "I will give away all my sins to know thee" (Alma 22:18).

If we were not carrying so much else, the cross would be lighter. Furthermore, we will not come to know God unless we do give away all our sins. This is part of losing and finding oneself. To whom shall we give our sins? Only Jesus is willing and able to take them.

The kind of things nonmurmurers are permitted to see should entice us. When his city was compassed about with "a great host" of hostile horses and chariots, Elisha counseled his anxious young servant, "Fear not: for they that be with us are more than they that be with them." The prophet then prayed that the Lord would "open the eyes" of the young man, "and he saw: and behold the mountain was full of horses and chariots of fire round about Elisha"! (2 Kings 6:14–17.)

Elisha's counsel can help to still our murmuring today: "Fear not: for they that be with us are more than they that be with them." If our lips are closed to murmuring our eyes can be opened.

All the ordinances of the gospel, directly and indirectly, can still our murmuring and likewise bear in one way or another upon the theme of remembrance; they also heighten anticipation.

All the big truths of the gospel take their place "fitly framed" in the order of daily life. They do not exist *apart* from life, but are interwoven with it. For instance, there is a God. He hears and answers our prayers. He knows what we will ask for even before we ask; our prayers are a petition. However, some mortals, if they pray at all, treat prayer as if God were the equivalent of a "911" emergency number. They forget the blessing but remember the number.

We can have known the big truths and then forgotten. But accountability remains even if memories are dimmed.

> But behold, when the time cometh that they shall dwindle in unbelief, after they have received so great blessings from the hand of the Lord—having a knowledge of the creation of the earth, and all men, knowing the great and marvelous works of the Lord from the creation of the world; having power given them to do all things by faith; having all the commandments from the beginning, and having been brought by his infinite goodness into this precious land of promise—behold, I say, if the day shall come that they will reject the Holy One of Israel, the true Messiah, their Redeemer and their God, behold, the judgments of him that is just shall rest upon them (2 Nephi 1:10).

We have meaning, as individuals, apart from our mortal roles and work. In the world to come one will not be known as a teacher, or a harness maker, or a secretary, or a mortician, or a policeman, or a housewife. The chores we do here are useful, some even essential. But there and then (and one would hope well before that) we will put away childish things, especially the toxic toys. Some skills no longer relevant will be discarded, too, like training wheels and water wings.

The Christian virtues, however, are both eternal and portable. They are never obsolete. They will always be relevant. Possessed of these in goodly measure, we will become, if faithful here, a man or a woman of God there.

This is all part of the fresh view of ourselves that we can have through the wonderful flood of light. There is much divine preparation under way, highly individualized preparation. Regarding the glorious potential future the Lord told the Apostle John: "To him that overcometh will I give to eat of the hidden manna, and will give him a white stone, and in the stone a new name written, which no man knoweth saving he that receiveth it" (Revelation 2:17). This white stone, wrote Joseph Smith, "will become a Urim and Thummim to each individual who receives one, whereby things pertaining to a higher order of kingdoms will be made known" (D&C 130:10).

Yet even with all the help now given to us and the supernal promises as to what lies ahead, there are stumbling blocks presently in our paths. These are real rocks of resistance to be overcome, and there can be much murmuring unless they are removed.

Chapter Five

"TAKING AWAY . . . STUMBLING BLOCKS"

Given human nature and our freedom to choose, or moral agency, plus the divinely designed proving and tutoring nature of mortal existence, the presence of stumbling blocks on the path to the development of faith should be no surprise (see D&C 76:53). But whether expected or unexpected, stumbling blocks are vexing—unless one is blessed with the wonderful flood of light that provides the illumination with which to see beyond them.

A stumbling block is defined as involving "something repugnant to one's prejudices" (*The Oxford English Dictionary*). One's prejudices or life's conditioning experiences can block the way to acceptance of a powerful and needed truth about things as they really are.

The Lord, perfectly perceiving human prejudices as these encrust mortal lives, describes His restored work as a "strange act" and "strange work" brought to pass so that men may discern "that which they have never considered" (D&C 101:94, 95).

A stumbling block of the Jews of Jesus' day, for instance, was their expectations about what the Messiah would do, such as emancipating them politically. To them, Jesus was not an emancipator, and his death was an unfulfilling stumbling block. This irony had been prophesied. The Greeks, on the other hand, regarded the whole idea of a resurrecting messiah as foolishness. (See Isaiah 8:14; 1 Corinthians 1:23; 1 Peter 2:8; 2 Nephi 18:14.)

In a way, stumbling blocks reflect the problem of perspective noted in scriptures about motes and beams. Some things seem larger than they are; others, not large enough. For many, the concept of revelation is a special stumbling block on the path leading to faith. The silence of the centuries of spiritual famine foreseen by Amos had led many to speak of the human connection as Peter foresaw: "All things continue as they were from the beginning" (2 Peter 3:4). The seeming sameness of it all leads to doubt and to a discounting of spiritual things.

The doctrine of revelation is intrinsically offensive to others who exclude from credibility any knowledge which is spiritually acquired. Thus this gospel doctrine of revelation is "repugnant to one's prejudices" for many moderns. Yet revelation is the only way of knowing certain transcendent things:

> Behold, great and marvelous are the works of the Lord. How unsearchable are the depths of the mysteries of him; and it is impossible that man should find out all his ways. And no man knoweth of his ways save it be revealed unto him; wherefore, brethren, despise not the revelations of God. . . .
>
> For the Spirit speaketh the truth and lieth not. Wherefore, it speaketh of things as they really are, and of things as they really will be. (Jacob 4:8, 13.)

As George MacDonald has written,

> No revelation can be other than partial. . . . For what revelation, other than a partial, can the highest spiritual condition receive of the infinite God? . . . the true revelation rouses the desire to know more by the truth of its incompleteness.

(George MacDonald, *Unspoken Sermons*, Series 1 [London: Alexander Strahan, 1867], pp. 35–36.)

For our Lord's arguments are for the presentation of the truth, and the truth carries its own conviction to him who is able to receive it (*Unspoken Sermons*, p. 18).

Sad, indeed, would the whole matter be, if the Bible had told us *everything* God had meant us to believe. But herein is the Bible itself greatly wronged. It nowhere lays claim to be regarded as *the* Word, *the* Way, *the* Truth. The Bible leads us to Jesus. . . . It is Christ "in whom are hid all the treasures of wisdom and knowledge," not the Bible, save as leading to him. (*Unspoken Sermons*, pp. 52–53.)

Every principle God has revealed carries its own convictions of its truth to the human mind (Brigham Young, *Journal of Discourses* 9:149).

The Lord does reveal Himself, truths, and elements of the future, but He does so *on His terms!* This is a divine constraint that makes for difficulties for the unmeek, because "the natural man receiveth not the things of the Spirit of God: for they are foolishness unto him: neither can he know them, because they are spiritually discerned" (1 Corinthians 2:14).

Some people expect—almost demand—that God will reveal himself on their terms and even according to their own schedule. Yet they would still reject God, especially if it should turn out that He resembles us mortals too much!

There are many who believe in some kind of God. Some believe in a god who has never declared his purposes clearly, a god who seems distant and preoccupied. Many likewise have a vague hope of some form of existence beyond the grave. Still others say that there once even was revelation from God, but certainly not in our time.

Not only was Jesus a stumbling block to the Jews and foolishness to the Greeks, but also Jesus' teachings offended many (see 1 Corinthians 1:23; Romans 9:33). Such ancient attitudes have their modern counterparts, because the things of the Spirit are still foolishness to the natural man. Jesus observed of

Himself and His work, "Blessed is he, whosoever shall not be offended in me" (Matthew 11:6).

Several illustrations of ancient antecedents follow, showing the firm exclusion of things "spiritually discerned" by revelation. First Sherem:

> No *man* knoweth of such things; for he *cannot tell of things to come* (Jacob 7:7, italics added).

Next Korihor:

> Why do ye look for a Christ? For *no man can know of anything which is to come....* How do ye know of their surety? Behold, *ye cannot know of things which ye do not see;* therefore ye cannot know that there shall be a Christ. (Alma 30:13; 15, italics added.)

The unbelieving Nephites:

> But behold, we know that this is a wicked tradition, ... to cause us that we should believe in some great and marvelous thing which should come to pass, but not among us, but in a land which is far distant, a land which we know not; therefore they can keep us in ignorance, for *we cannot witness with our own eyes that they are true* (Helaman 16:20, italics added).

Laman:

> Now, [Nephi] *says* that the Lord has talked with him, and also that *angels have ministered unto* him. But behold, *we know that he lies unto us* (1 Nephi 16:38, italics added).

The resulting view of life is one-dimensional, being fed by doubts of and disbelief in immortality: "And thus [Korihor] did preach unto them, leading away the hearts of many, causing them to lift up their heads in their wickedness, yea, leading away many women, and also men, to commit whoredoms — telling them that *when a man was dead, that was the end thereof*" (Alma 30:18, italics added).

In sum, many maintain that we simply cannot know the future; that angels do not minister to man; and furthermore that we cannot accept the word of those who testify otherwise! For some this amounts to an article of faith: "We find insufficient evidence for belief in the existence of a supernatural; it is either meaningless or irrelevant to the question of the survival and fulfillment of the human race. As non-theists, we begin with humans not God, nature not deity. . . . No deity will save us; we must save ourselves." (Humanist Manifesto II, *Encyclopedia of American Religions: Religions Creeds*, J. Gordon Melton, ed. [Detroit: Gale Research Company, 1988], p. 641.)

Fortunately, as Latter-day Saints we know better, having been blessed with the witness of the Spirit. We recognize that the development of one's spiritual capacity is not only possible but also vital. The various human senses are prized and useful. These are interactive, but they are also individualized. We do not use our ears to smell, our eyes to taste, or our noses to hear. We do not expect one sense to do the work of another. Similarly, the highly valued scientific method has its own yield—its own ways of discovering and knowing. But it is to be pursued on its own terms, and when it is, much benefit can result.

It is so too with "the things of the Spirit." These are spiritually discerned—that is, they yield to the methodology of the Spirit. (1 Corinthians 2:14; see also Romans 8:5.) In its own way the Spirit provides individual verification as the individual observes certain conditions, thereby even offering a form of needed "reproduceability."

To exclude revelation as a way of gaining knowledge is to exclude certain vital truths altogether—truths revealed over the long span of religious history. The historical pattern of revelation in fact goes back to the beginning:

> And after God had appointed that these things should come unto man, behold, then he saw that it was expedient that man should know concerning the things whereof he had appointed unto them;
> Therefore he sent angels to converse with them, who caused men to behold of his glory.

And they began from that time forth to call on his name; therefore God conversed with men, and made known unto them the plan of redemption, which had been prepared from the foundation of the world; and this he made known unto them according to their faith and repentance and their holy works. (Alma 12:28–30.)

Noteworthy are Alma's words that "it was expedient that man should know concerning the things whereof [God] had appointed unto them" (Alma 12:28). This is precisely the perspective—God's plans for men—that mortals need and that Laman and Lemuel did not have. They murmured "because they knew not the dealings of that God who had created them" (1 Nephi 2:12). Without a view of eternity, we can easily misread the daily things; thus the fresh view brought by the Restoration brings a change of mind and becomes crucial for us all in daily life!

For those meek enough to consider it, one way in which the stumbling block of doubt concerning revelation can be removed is by examining and then acknowledging the fruits of the Restoration, which are explainable only through revelation. This was the purport of the angel's words to Nephi. "And it shall come to pass, that if the Gentiles shall hearken unto the Lamb of God in that day that he shall manifest himself unto them in word, and also in power, in very deed, unto the taking away of their stumbling blocks—" (1 Nephi 14:1).

Searching out and seeing the blending of the truths and witnesses of the Bible and the Book of Mormon (not possible for Joseph Smith to have managed) is another way to remove the doubts about revelation. The Lord told Joseph of Egypt:

Wherefore, the fruit of thy loins shall write; and the fruit of the loins of Judah shall write; and that which shall be written by the fruit of thy loins, and also that which shall be written by the fruit of the loins of Judah, shall grow together, unto the confounding of false doctrines and laying down of contentions, and establishing peace among the fruit of thy loins, and bringing them to the knowledge of their fathers in the latter days, and also to the knowledge of my covenants, saith the Lord (2 Nephi 3:12).

The growing together of Bible and Book of Mormon helps establish the truth of both books.

God foresaw the sweeping skepticism of our time, but He also provided ways out! The miraculous miracle which resumed the ancient pattern is really explainable in only one way. Just as occurred to others in the beginning of religious history, visitations to Joseph Smith were made by many heavenly messengers, bringing vital knowledge concerning God and His plans and purposes. "Wherefore, I the Lord, knowing the calamity which should come upon the inhabitants of the earth, called upon my servant Joseph Smith, Jun., and spake unto him from heaven, and gave him commandments" (D&C 1:17).

There were many angels at the dedication of the Kirtland Temple on March 27, 1836. The Prophet elsewhere refers to "divers angels . . . from Michael or Adam down to the present time" (D&C 128:20-21). Those heavenly visitors were not mute. Joseph was ordained by them, received keys from them, and was instructed and directed by them.

Thus vital missing truths have been restored by revelation, but only for those who will believe: "And now, Moses, my son, . . . in a day when the children of men shall esteem my words as naught and take many of them from the book which thou shalt write, behold, I will raise up another like unto thee; and they shall be had again among the children of men—*among as many as shall believe.*" (Moses 1:40-41, italics added.)

It is unfortunate that for most the stumbling block regarding revelation remains. Many mortals simply exclude spiritual things. Nor can those who receive revelation share indiscriminately all they have received:

> And now Alma began to expound these things unto him, saying: It is given unto many to know the mysteries of God; nevertheless they are laid under a strict command that they shall not impart only according to the portion of his word

which he doth grant unto the children of men, according to the heed and diligence which they give unto him.

And therefore, he that will harden his heart, the same receiveth the lesser portion of the word; and he that will not harden his heart, to him is given the greater portion of the word, until it is given unto him to know the mysteries of God until he know them in full.

And they that will harden their hearts, to them is given the lesser portion of the word until they know nothing concerning his mysteries; and then they are taken captive by the devil, and led by his will down to destruction. Now this is what is meant by the chains of hell. (Alma 12:9–11; see also Matthew 13:10–13; 16:20; 3 Nephi 28:11, 18; Ether 13:13; Helaman 4:12; D&C 6:12; 41:6.)

Paul sums up the concept that what we truly focus on determines what we will see: "For they that are after the flesh do mind the things of the flesh; but they that are after the Spirit the things of the Spirit" (Romans 8:5).

Another stumbling block for some mortals is the seeming injustice of God. We naturally recoil from the jarring examples of the human condition with its many injustices, insensitivities, inequalities, and immense sufferings. Surely, however, we dare not assume that our anguish reflects a more highly developed sense of empathy for humanity than God Himself has! Yet the stone of stumbling is there. Says George MacDonald: "I suspect a great part of our irreligion springs from our disbelief in the humanity of God" (George MacDonald, *The Miracles of Our Lord* [London: Strahan and Co., 1870], p. 265).

In fact, many things show that our God is just and merciful. It is God who has given us dozens upon dozens of urgings concerning our responsibilities to the poor, including the word that poverty can destroy opportunities for education (3 Nephi 6:12). It is He, however, who had told us that the real remedy for poverty requires that things be done in His own way (see D&C 104:15–16). Poverty will not be cured by mortal bandaids. The same Lord who criticized Sodom because of their gross sexual immorality also lamented that they grossly neglected their poor (see Ezekiel 16:49).

It is God who has warned us of the great inequality that occurs because of sin (see D&C 49:20).

It is He who has told us that it is not right that one man should be in bondage to another (see D&C 101:79).

It is He who has warned us about how very few people can handle power properly and riches properly (see D&C 121:39; Luke 18:24–25).

It is He who, from the beginning, has beckoned us, His children, to return to Him, yet we can choose either liberty or captivity, for as he told Adam, "nevertheless, thou mayest choose for thyself" (Moses 3:17). We have our moral agency (see D&C 101:78).

It is He who, through the redemption of His Son, Jesus Christ, has prepared for the billions and billions of mortals three post-resurrection kingdoms of glory. It is He who rejoiced in those brief periods (see 4 Nephi) when people were truly righteous, and when there "could not be a happier people." It was He who guided the formation of the righteous and remarkable city of Enoch and who wept over the condition of the wicked (see Moses 7:28).

It is He who has told us He delights to honor those who serve Him (see D&C 76:5).

It is He—just and merciful—who has told us that the workers in the vineyard who come in the last hour shall receive the same wages as those laboring from the very first hour (see Matthew 20:1–16). It will be so because of the "goodman of the house."

Notwithstanding all his concern for his children, God, being just, merciful, and wise, did not initiate the plan of salvation, with its conditions essential to growth, only to suspend it when the going gets rough. He did not give us moral agency merely to withdraw it, because He desires for us the greater happiness it brings us. He, much more than we, must endure the suffering of His children. His work and glory is to bring to pass the immortality and eternal life of man (see Moses 1:39). But it will be accomplished in his own due time and in his own way (D&C 88:68; D&C 24:16; 136:18; D&C 64:32). And since His ways are so much higher than man's ways (see Isaiah 55:9), we must not expect to judge them by our mortal reasoning but rather accept them with faith and trust in Him.

The Lord will surely stay the course. The only question is, will we?

As we have seen, we cannot properly charge God with being insufficiently sensitive to human suffering. Instead let us do what we can within our circles of influence to remedy human suffering but without forgetting the tie between agency and misery (as well as between agency and happiness) and certain of life's overarching purposes. Indeed, the reality that "there is an opposition in all things" (2 Nephi 2:11) may mean that Murphy's Law (anything that *can* go wrong *will* go wrong) is a vexing subset of that reality.

What we should *not* do is magnify our sufferings instead of our callings by having an exaggerated sense of those sufferings, real and intense as these are at times. An extreme case is Sidney Rigdon, who—swollen with self-pity—said while in Liberty Jail "that the sufferings of Jesus Christ were a fool to his" (Keith W. Perkins, "Trials and Tribulations: The Refiner's Fire," in *The Capstone of Our Religion*, Robert L. Millet and Larry E. Dahl, eds. [Salt Lake City: Bookcraft, 1989], p. 147).

Keith Perkins observed of this moment of truth: "After this experience he [Sidney Rigdon] was no longer the great leader of the Church that he had been. Joseph Smith no longer wanted him as a counselor because of his unfaithfulness; the Prophet later remarked that if Sidney Rigdon led the Church he 'would lead the Church to destruction in less than five years.' " (In *Capstone*, p. 147.)

The slide of Sidney Rigdon—all the way out of the kingdom—brought this response of remembrance from Brigham Young, showing empathy for Sidney Rigdon but also Brigham's firm principles:

> I am willing that you should know that my feelings for Sidney Rigdon as a man, as a private citizen, are of the best kind. I have loved that man and always had the very best feelings for him; I have stood in defense of his life and his house in

Kirtland, and have lain on the floor, night after night, and week after week, to defend him. There are those who are following Sidney for whom my heart is grieved, I esteem them as good citizens. But when it touches the salvation of the people, I am the man that walks to the line. (Brigham Young, quoted in *Times and Seasons*, September 15, 1844, p. 648.)

Few episodes show God's empathy more than the colloquy with Enoch. Enoch was puzzled over how the Lord (who had created many earths besides this one, resulting in numberless creations by our reckoning, and who was surrounded by holiness, peace, justice, truth, and mercy) could weep. Enoch, full of empathy for mankind, nevertheless asked the Lord, "How is it that thou canst weep?"

The Lord replied that Enoch's contemporaries were among the very "workmanship of [his own] hands." He had given them their moral agency and a commandment to love one another. But "behold, they are without affection, and they hate their own blood"; and their wickedness was great. Thus viewing the lack of love and the abundance of sin, the Lord's reply to Enoch was: "Wherefore should not the heavens weep, seeing these shall suffer?" The weeping was over the status quo, but especially since these individuals were going to suffer in torment until the redemption occurred! So the Lord again responded to Enoch's question, "Wherefore, for this shall the heavens weep."

Then the Lord told Enoch "all the doings of the children of men . . . their wickedness, and their misery." Then it was Enoch's turn to weep, "and his heart swelled wide as eternity." At first, Enoch refused to be comforted. But he was shown the atoning day of the Lord! (Moses 7:29-67.)

No one can read this supernal revelatory account without feeling the divine tenderness of God's sharing in human suffering. In view of this, praise be to God for His long-suffering and patience! Our Father and our Redeemer are perfect in both their mercy and their justice—and divine empathy bridges those two virtues. "In all their affliction he was afflicted, and the angel of his presence saved them: in his love and in his pity he redeemed them; and he bare them, and carried them all the days of old" (Isaiah 63:9).

Lacking gospel light or ignoring gospel perspective, we create many of our own problems. Those who desire complexity instead of simplicity can surely complicate simple things. Those who insist on "looking beyond the mark"—the obvious—are those most likely to trip over stumbling blocks, as the Jews were anciently:

> But behold, the Jews were a stiffnecked people; and they despised the words of plainness, and killed the prophets, and sought for things that they could not understand. Wherefore, because of their blindness, which blindness came by looking beyond the mark, they must needs fall; for God hath taken away his plainness from them, and delivered unto them many things which they cannot understand, because they desired it. And because they desired it God hath done it, that they may stumble. (Jacob 4:14.)

Just as one can experience temporary blindness by staring at the glare of sun-drenched snow, one can likewise stare into ambiguity and incomprehensibility too long. Then the plainness which is near at hand goes unseen. Squinting to see past plainness and beyond the obvious causes some to end up "looking beyond the mark," thus tripping over even the smallest stumbling blocks.

Blindness can be cultural as well as individual: "For I would not, brethren, that ye should be ignorant of this mystery, . . . that blindness in part is happened to Israel, until the fulness of the Gentiles be come in" (Romans 11:25).

Thus the wonderful flood of light of the restored gospel is so essential in order that we may have a fresh view and thereby change our minds and our behavior. This individual increase of light, this progress continues as we seek it: "That which is of God is light; and he that receiveth light, and continueth in God, receiveth more light; and that light groweth brighter and brighter until the perfect day" (D&C 50:24; see also Matthew 6:22).

Meanwhile, many things can obscure our view of reality or can block our spiritual memories.

Another stubborn block is that, in Wordsworth's words, "the world is too much with us." We are not only diverted, sometimes we are almost fixated by temporal and lesser but pressing things. This stumbling block includes the diverting satisfactions that go with the "joy for a season" flowing from men's accomplishments. We can, wrote Paul, pursue "foolish and hurtful lusts, which drown men" (1 Timothy 6:9).

The cares and anxieties of the world occupy us as if we were children making dikes and castles on the beach, unaware that each day's incoming surf will erase our sincere but temporal labors.

In keeping with Nephi's prophecy (2 Nephi 28:8) there exists also the mistaken and hindering notion that God will "beat us with a few stripes" and all will still be well. This expectation of an "easy fix" blocks many of us from doing the hard things. This particular stumbling block is most often encountered at the border between casual and serious discipleship. Many not only are detained by it but also come to rest in its rooms of rationalization.

There are still others who stumble simply because they are jaded or bored. Their "yawns are a silent shout" from being oppressed by the "hum-drum nihilism." Boredom causes people to "die as to things pertaining unto righteousness" (Alma 12:16). Would that such souls could emulate the prodigal, who finally "came to himself" and returned to his father (Luke 15:17, 20). One cannot be laid back and still press forward. To "awake to righteousness" requires us to "awake and arouse [our] faculties" and to "awake to a remembrance" and to dispel the "cloud of darkness," so that we, like Lamoni, can be "lit up in [the] soul." (1 Corinthians 15:34; Alma 32:27; Mosiah 2:40; Alma 19:6.)

Another stumbling block for some is the fact that, in their perception, the vast majority of humans have never heard and will never hear the gospel of Jesus Christ; and how can a just God judge mortals who are deprived of this important knowledge? What they do not understand is that God has made "ample provision." He has supplied not only the needed Savior but also a spiritual safety net for those who died without a knowledge of the gospel or who died in infancy. Thus all who would have sincerely received the gospel had they heard it in mortality will receive the same rewards as those who did hear it here and lived by it. Their receiving of equivalent and ultimate blessings shows the justice and mercy of God. "All who have died without a knowledge of this gospel, who would have received it if they had been permitted to tarry, shall be heirs of the celestial kingdom of God: also all that shall die henceforth without a knowledge of it, who would have received it with all their hearts, shall be heirs of that kingdom" (D&C 137:7–8).

This soaring promise, fulfilled in part by vicarious ordinances in holy temples, applies to many millions of souls, such as those who lived in the Middle Ages out of reach of the Restoration. In God's mercy there is a plan for all and a place for each. This particular doctrine removes a major stumbling block for those who view the sweep of the centuries as evidence of God's injustice. As a church we do not fully appreciate the emancipatory, as well as the revelatory, significance of the above verses.

We are similarly assured concerning all the children who die before the age of accountability: they are heirs to the celestial kingdom (see D&C 137:10). The mercy of God is not at the mercy of infant mortality. Elder John A. Widtsoe further observed: "Those who die before the age of accountability have their bodies. If in their pre-existent state they have not made themselves unworthy, it is not thinkable that they will be deprived of any blessing held in reserve for the saints of God. They will be in the hands of the Lord, who is full of love and justice. We may safely leave them there." (John A. Widtsoe, *Evidences and Reconciliations*, vol. 1 [Salt Lake City: Bookcraft, 1943], p. 279.)

Hence the Father's arm of mercy has been extended to those in various dispensations. He keeps trying to communicate with those who have ears to hear, whether on this side of the veil of death or the other.

Certain powerful verses of scripture that, for the present,

seem to slumber as if in the Church's unconscious will also come to the fore to push aside still other stumbling blocks. These await the blossoming moment of our collective understanding or the marshaling moment of collective undertaking.

One such verse concerns human, economic inequality; it stresses the destabilizing effects of poverty: "But it is not given that one man should possess that which is above another, wherefore the world lieth in sin" (D&C 49:20). The time of our deeper, collective appreciation of the gospel's response to this particular challenge is not yet, but it will come. The interplay of agency and poverty are finally resolvable only through the fulness of the gospel by those willing to do things in the Lord's own way (see D&C 104:16).

There are many who are genuinely contributive and who lead decent lives even though they genuinely believe that "when a man [is] dead, that [is] the end thereof" (Alma 30:18). These individuals do not stumble so much as simply and sincerely halt their journey of faith short of where they might have gone. This severe stumbling occurs because of life's seeming pointlessness for those who see things without the eye of faith.

Actually, God has carefully designed this life according to His announced and stern specifications, which include letting us use our moral agency (see D&C 136:3; Mosiah 23:21; Deuteronomy 8:2; Abraham 3:25; D&C 98:12). Should we choose to live without God in the world and without knowledge of those design specifications, it is quite likely that we will comment critically. All feel those stern specifications, even those who do not acknowledge the Architect; and the latter tend to multiply their murmuring.

Some who do not acknowledge God—and, for that matter, some who do—proceed through life insensitively. Like Korihor, they apparently believe that in this life we fare only according to the individual management of the creature, and that everyone conquers according to his genius or strength (see Alma 30:17). To the "strong," this seems ideal, but what of the conquered and subdued? Injustice multiplies like insects in the sunshine.

Because of stumbling blocks, some people simply and sincerely throw in with prevailing scientism, turning away from exploration of the realm of religion.

The scientific method is so useful to mankind in many ways. It focuses on the available data concerning the *how* and *what* of things, but it leaves to the individual the answering of the *why* questions. In any case, there is assumed to be a paucity of data concerning these questions, and a further assumption is that stereotyped religion is not a significant source of such data. Hence other data are looked to. Stephen W. Hawking writes: "Up to now, most scientists have been too occupied with the development of new theories that describe *what* the universe is to ask the question *why*. On the other hand, the people whose business it is to ask *why*, the philosophers, have not been able to keep up with the advance of scientific theories."

The large and haunting questions of *why* still brood ominously over the human scene. Some are hopeful: "However, if we do discover a complete theory, it should in time be understandable in broad principle by everyone, not just a few scientists. Then we shall all, philosophers, scientists, and just ordinary people, be able to take part in the discussion of the question of why it is that we and the universe exist. If we find the answer to that, it would be the ultimate triumph of human reason—for then we would know the mind of God." (Stephen W. Hawking, *A Brief History of Time* [New York: Bantam Books, 1988], pp. 174, 175.)

A further and great stumbling block is the human inability to endure well. When we come to see things with a correct view, we will see, for instance, that those sufferings which are "common to man" (1 Corinthians 10:13) provide no exemptions or immunities. We will also see that some suffering involves customized tutoring, given for our own good (see D&C 122:7). It is thought that in the premortal world some may have even agreed to accept suffering here. While much of the suffering simply cannot be explained at present, in all situations, whatever their nature, we are to endure well and to hold out (see 2 Nephi 31:16; D&C 122:9; 121:8; 6:13). We are to have faith in God, which involves the special trust that goes with waiting—waiting sometimes without answers, or waiting for an illness to pass or to finally claim us. But how does one so perform if he believes his God is indifferent or unable to do His work?

This underscores the great serviceability of the quality of endurance. We do not need to incessantly ask *why?* but perhaps only *how long?*

It is striking that on one of the rare occasions when we have the direct and testifying words of the Father they concerned the importance of enduring. Nephi reported: "And I heard a voice from the Father, saying: Yea, the words of my Beloved are true and faithful. He that endureth to the end, the same shall be saved." (2 Nephi 31:15; see also 2 Nephi 31:20.)

The remedies for people who stumble because they feel unvalued, unloved, unused, unheeded, and unappreciated include coming to know about God's love and coming to see the disappointments of the day in the context of the blessings of eternity and God's plan of happiness. It is vital for one to know that life's real difficulties are "but for a small moment" and thereby to trust in God's timing (see D&C 122:4; 2 Corinthians 4:17). Likewise, with the fresh view that comes from Restoration light we realize that our qualities and gifts are portable and will go with us into the next world. These qualities and gifts may not have been adequately appreciated here, but they are much in demand there!

Our suffering, of course, comes from a mixture of our mistakes, the mistakes of others, complex circumstances, and inexplicabilities. Try as we may to sort all these out, there are often too many factors and too many imponderables. But even though we do not know "the meaning of all things" we can still know that God "loveth his children" (1 Nephi 11:17).

Even so, we must know that we are the focus of the Lord's work. He has His own schedule, however, and will do certain things "in [his] own due time" (D&C 42:62; 59:4; 64:32). The various episodes in scriptures provide precious perspective. One focus on a particular challenge to the Church was spread over some time. When officers serving the Jewish leaders indicated their favorable impression of Jesus and his teachings, "Then answered them the Pharisees, Are ye also deceived? Have any of the rulers or of the Pharisees believed on him?" (John 7:47–48.) Months later, however, "among the chief rulers also many believed on him; but because of the Pharisees they did not confess him, lest they should be put out of the synagogue: for they loved the praise of men more than the praise of God" (John 12:42–43). And still later, "the word of God increased; and the number of the disciples multiplied in Jerusalem greatly; and a great company of the priests were obedient to the faith" (Acts 6:7).

Another stumbling block, surprising in a way, is man's very capacity and opportunity to choose. Without recognizing the stone for what it is, some truly stumble over the major role of free agency within the plan of salvation. Wrong choices do produce much human tragedy and suffering; therefore, we might like to have "the voice of an angel" to affect the choosing of others. But Jesus' message is one of invitation, not intimidation. As free volunteers, we can't keep ourselves or others on the strait and narrow path by the tyranny of even that trumpet.

How ancient is this pattern of our choosing? It clearly existed in the first estate, where God obviously permitted us to choose. "For behold, the devil . . . rebelled against me, saying, Give me thine honor, which is my power; and also a third part of the hosts of heaven turned he away from me because of their agency" (D&C 29:36).

God's commitment to our freedom is of greater length and depth than we ever have imagined. He affirmed our agency again in the Garden (see Moses 7:32). In the mortal garden, men can choose "of every tree." But, as in the other garden, we are advised to avoid certain things.

The scriptures make it clear how powerful and essential is this gift of agency: "All truth is independent in that sphere in which God has placed it, to act for itself, as all intelligence also; otherwise there is no existence. Behold, here is the agency of man, and here is the condemnation of man; because that which was from the beginning is plainly manifest unto them, and they receive not the light." (D&C 93:30–31.)

We are left to "do according to [our] own will" (Mosiah 2:21) so "that every man may act in doctrine and principle pertaining to futurity, according to the moral agency which I have given unto him, that every man may be accountable for his own sins in the day of judgment" (D&C 101:78).

We have agency, and life provides alternatives and opportunities from which to choose—all in order for us to grow. Otherwise, our existence would be a "compound in one," an undifferentiated lump of insensibility.

There had to be "an opposition" in all things. Without such opposition there would be no righteousness, no wickedness, no holiness, no misery, nothing that was good, nothing that was bad. All things would be that seemingly inert "compound in one." We would be as if dead, with no sense or insensibility. There would be no purpose in the end of our creation! (See 2 Nephi 2:11.)

The above scriptural pairings tell us much. In the listing of holiness and misery as opposites, the absence of holiness means the presence of misery! Likewise, the more holiness, the more happiness. Hence, "More holiness give me" ("More Holiness Give Me," *Hymns*, no. 131).

Our task, then, is to "choose the right when a choice is placed before [us]" ("Choose the Right," *Hymns*, no. 239). We have had that privilege of choosing, however, for a long, long time!

Granted, there are times when things get very bad, as in Sodom and Gomorrah or in the days of Noah. Then the Lord acts! President John Taylor said of the wickedness of Sodom and Gomorrah: "It was better for [the inhabitants] to die, and thus be deprived of their agency, which they abused, than entail so much misery on their posterity, and bring ruin upon millions of unborn persons" (John Taylor, *The Government of God* [Liverpool: S. W. Richards, 1852], p. 53).

The long-suffering of God does not strive with man interminably (see D&C 1:33; Genesis 6:3).

The Lord wants us to be forgiving, however (see D&C 64:9–10), thus providing support and welcome for the repentant individual. God knows whether or not the repentance is sincere, but to us it is given to "continue to minister" even to the unheeding because we "know not but what they will return and repent" (3 Nephi 18:32).

Enduring and forgiving provide us with much-needed experience. And experience, after all, is one major reason why we have come to earth to pass through our second estate.

We seem to learn some things best by experience:

> And Laban said unto him, I pray thee, if I have found favour in thine eyes, tarry: for I have learned by experience that the Lord hath blessed me for thy sake (Genesis 30:27).

> We have learned by sad experience that it is the nature and disposition of almost all men, as soon as they get a little authority, as they suppose, they will immediately begin to exercise unrighteous dominion (D&C 121:39).

> If the very jaws of hell shall gape open the mouth wide after thee, know thou, my son, that all these things shall give thee experience, and shall be for thy good (D&C 122:7).

> That my people may be taught more perfectly, and have experience, and know more perfectly concerning their duty, and the things which I require at their hands (D&C 105:10).

Experience not only helps us come to know things for ourselves but it also makes the precious process of remembrance possible.

Enduring brings such a rich supply of experience, of opportunities to use our moral agency, especially when we take Jesus' yoke upon us in order to learn of Him in an accelerated way: "Take my yoke upon you, and learn of me; for I am meek and lowly in heart; and ye shall find rest unto your souls" (Matthew 11:29).

Experience, however, cannot be rushed. Experience requires time. And time requires patience.

The gospel's answers to the big *why* of life help us answer the little *whys*. We can then better keep going even when bruised, battered, and bleeding. Like Jesus, though on our tiny scale, we are to continue until "it is finished" (see John 19:30).

One day God will "wipe away tears from off all faces" (Isaiah 25:8). After all, "we are the people of his pasture, and the sheep of his hand" (Psalm 95:7).

Meanwhile, to develop an "eye single" will help us to see stumbling blocks for what they really are. That focused eye will also see that the basic truths are so simple and yet so stunning —for example, that "all the planets which move in their regular form do witness that there is a Supreme Creator" (Alma 30:44), and that "all things are created and made to bear record of [Jesus Christ]" (Moses 6:63).

We will see, for instance, divine design not only in the galaxies but also in the minute, double helix of the DNA molecule's marvelous order and beauty!

True, some observe such ordering beauty without assigning credit to God, and they are left free so to conclude (see Isaiah 45:9). Perhaps some such fear being "taken in" should they believe in a God and thus go against conventional, agnostic wisdom. Or perhaps some are simply too busy discovering the trees to ponder the forest—the large, strategic questions, such as "Why?" There are those thoughtful scientists, however, who, having considered *how* the universe came into being, *what* it is composed of, believe in God.

But of all the stumbling blocks, personal sins are clearly the largest and most retarding. Before we can receive all that God has for us, we must first make room by giving away our sins.

Chapter Six

"Give Away All My Sins to Know Thee"

As our view of things as they really are becomes clearer by reason of the Restoration's wonderful flood of light, our desire to change and to improve becomes stronger. So far as our individual spiritual development is concerned, we usually know what we have to give up, what has to go. Why then do we cling so tenaciously to those things?

Is it because, deep down, we really think God will only beat us with a few stripes and then quickly forget our sins? (2 Nephi 28:8.) Do we think our good works are more than enough to compensate for our few frailties? Do we think the things we cling to are not really so bad after all? Or do we cling to certain things simply because everybody else seems to have a few personal deficiencies too?

Only an eye that is becoming single to the glory of God will keep us conscious of our beams and even our remaining motes. Such illumination brings the restlessness of incipient righteousness. And we reach a point at which we genuinely say, as did King Lamoni's father, "I am willing to give away all my sins to know [God]" (see Alma 22:18).

In this situation, the cleaner we become, the more conscious we are of the remaining dirt. Like remarkable Peter, we may be essentially "clean, but not all" (John 13:10). Cleansing circumstances are to be welcomed even if the scrubbing is painful.

An eye not single is a dangerous eye, "for although a man may have many revelations, and have power to do many mighty works, yet if he boasts in his own strength, and sets at naught the counsels of God, and follows after the dictates of his own will and carnal desires, he must fall and incur the vengeance of a just God upon him" (D&C 3:4).

Not only can an unsingle eye result in an obscuring of our view of certain things but it also means that we are giving off less light even though more individual illumination is always and urgently needed (see D&C 88:67).

An incomplete view of things can also cause us to turn into complainers (Jude 1:16; 1 Nephi 2:12). Furthermore, any blockage might cause us to scoff at sacred things or even at the servants of the Lord (see 2 Peter 3:3).

If we indulge in lust, this can "choke the word" (Mark 4:19). As with Cain or with Laban (see Moses 5:31–33; 1 Nephi 3:25), the lust might be for property and riches. "But they that will be rich fall into temptation and a snare, and into many foolish and hurtful lusts, which drown men in destruction and perdition" (1 Timothy 6:9). This is one reason why we are told to "seek not for riches but for wisdom" (D&C 6:7).

Not only does lust choke the word but so also do the incessant cares of the world, especially if we become "overcharged" with them (see Matthew 13:22; Luke 21:34).

Unchecked lusts do not usually exist in isolation but instead will probably drive one to seek the company of the like-minded, who even recruit teachers specializing in the curriculum of concupiscence (see 2 Timothy 4:3). In any such group, whether formal or informal, the risks of retaining our sins are great.

Though we should be willing to "give away all [our] sins," some sins seem especially hard for us to give away. For instance, it may be hard for us to give up our comfortable and established dominance of other humans. Even if it is not malicious, this subordination, this putting others down, can give us a false lift. Such predictable and unredemptive relationships will make it difficult for us to be meek in all circumstances.

For some it may be difficult to give up a particular form of lasciviousness which, though expressed only in marriage, is not proper. Disciples are to be different, however, living "not in the lust of concupiscence" (1 Thessalonians 4:5).

We may have a particular "toy," a childish thing or activity which is difficult for us to "put away." Whatever it is, it has come to mean too much to us. Such holding back holds us back spiritually.

It may be hard for us to give up praise or place in the world's establishments, especially if that place is earned and deserved.

It may be difficult for us to give up a particular gripe, or an issue for which our clever murmuring has almost become a trademark. We could end up as residents in a compound of complainers almost without noticing it. To walk away from such a pattern may involve the biggest steps we have ever taken!

The sin we are reluctant to give away may be nonlethal. Nevertheless our failure to jettison it keeps us from a measure of our real tasks.

Activities that are personally renewing are very appropriate when properly kept in place. By renewing us, these can help us to serve better. But, like riches, they must be pursued secondarily (see Jacob 2:18–19). If our eye is not becoming ever more single, seeking to "build up" the kingdom of God, it is dangerous to "give place" to such pursuits. Even harmless hobbies must be kept in their confined place, or they can take over.

Unconditional surrender of our shortcomings, on the other hand, brings us unforeseen opportunities for service by providing the optimum conditions for our personal growth. In fact, unconditional surrender to God is actually a personal victory!

Such surrender is giving up squinting through a homemade telescope in exchange for a chance to see things as they really are. This fresh view made possible by this dispensation's flood of light is made more breathtaking by our using an eye single to the glory of God.

This surrender is giving up our hovel, which we have cobbled together in the earthly slums, in exchange for a celestial mansion on the hill.

It is giving up the headaches that go with intense selfishness in exchange for being able to focus all of one's mind on Him and on His cause. This relief from recurring spasms of selfishness produces its own special form of rest (see Matthew 11:28).

It is also leaving the church of selfishness with its solitary member in exchange for belonging to a genuine community of saints.

Why, therefore, the resistance to such surrender? There is one particular reason among many. When citing the scripture about losing oneself and finding oneself, we often fail to take into account the vital, preceding verse:

> Then said Jesus unto his disciples, If any man will come after me, let him deny himself, and take up his cross, and follow me.
>
> For whosoever will save his life shall lose it: and whosoever will lose his life for my sake shall find it.
>
> For what is a man profited, if he shall gain the whole world, and lose his own soul? or what shall a man give in exchange for his soul? (Matthew 16:24–26.)

But what are we first to deny ourselves? Verse 26 in the Joseph Smith Translation reads: "And now for a man to take up his cross, is to deny himself all ungodliness, and every worldly lust, and keep my commandments." The "giving away" of all of one's sins is a preceding and accompanying condition to losing oneself for the Savior's sake. Unless we give away those wrong things we cannot "give place" for the seed of faith to grow (see Alma 32:27). The crowding cares of the world will constrain the things of the Spirit (see Luke 8:14).

This need for particularized denial is also strongly emphasized in the directions given by the resurrected Jesus:

> Behold, it is written by them of old time, that thou shalt not commit adultery;
> But I say unto you, that whosoever looketh on a woman, to lust after her, hath committed adultery already in his heart.
> Behold, I give unto you a commandment, that ye suffer none of these things to enter into your heart;
> For it is better that ye should deny yourselves of these things, wherein ye will take up your cross, than that ye should be cast into hell. (3 Nephi 12:27–30.)

Mental as well as physical adultery are especially mentioned as being among "these things." Therefore, losing our lust is part of losing ourselves for the Savior's sake. Losing the burden of our lust makes possible the taking up of the cross.

The forming of discipleship is like the forming of friendship, about which Boswell wrote: "We cannot tell the precise moment when friendship is formed. As in filling a vessel drop by drop, there is at last a drop which makes it run over; so in a series of kindnesses, there is at last one which makes the heart run over." (James Boswell, *Life of Johnson* [Oxford: Oxford University Press, 1980], p. 848.) Yes, there are identifiable, measurable, and initial turning points, but discipleship's development is deed by deed and thought by thought—along with the giving away, one after another, of our sins.

The fulness flowing from Restoration scriptures thus provides a much more complete picture of what is required in the losing-finding sequence. Without that picture, too many of us try to serve God and man while still indulging ourselves. Jesus goes to the very heart of the matter, showing that full service to God and others requires full personal integrity. The person, halved by hypocrisy into his public and private portions, must first find his true self.

There is the additional point that commandment keepers, undiminished by gross sin, have so much more of themselves to give!

Lest we rationalize the indulging of ourselves, holding on to ungodly things because these seem so private, we have only to look at Sodom and Gomorrah to see what cumulative misery consenting adults caused through their so-called victimless crimes!

Ambivalence diminishes as sins are given away. Otherwise, even though he gains the world of music through composing significant songs, a composer who goes rutting about while neglecting his wife and family has broken their tender hearts (see Jacob 2:35) even though putting musical notes together. In the family's next generation, tragic anger or imitation may be acted out. The music which flows from such a composer cannot compensate fully for his folly. In eternal perspective, a soothing symphony does not compensate for jarring cacaphony in personal conduct. Besides, better music is ahead (see 1 Corinthians 2:9).

A philanthropist may "gain" worldly acclaim by dispensing his largesse. If, at the same time, he is engaging in hanky-panky with other funds, he has lost his integrity of soul.

An athlete may "gain the whole world" as to sports records, but by failing to deny himself drugs he becomes a "castaway" (1 Corinthians 9:27). Castaways of all types have cast away the cross in their eagerness to gain the whole world.

An otherwise successful politician can be unsuccessful in preventing his addiction to earthly power while the powers of heaven were in fact accessible to him.

How can we possibly lose ourselves, anyway, if we withhold some of ourselves? How can we lose ourselves if, even in small ways, we go on indulging ourselves in ungodly things? This is not unconditional surrender to God. Hence to deny oneself "all ungodliness" is a vital test.

To withhold some of oneself brings subtle consequences. There is always the irrevocable loss of misspent time. Time spent in indulging oneself cannot be spent simultaneously in other ways. We cannot engage in murmuring and use that same time for praising. We cannot engage in griping at the very time we are consoling others.

Each moment belongs either to us or to God!

Though not yet fully worthy we are actually of enormous value, for "the worth of souls is great" (D&C 18:10). Yet compared to all that God has done for us we are by that measure still "unprofitable servants." Several scriptures portray people exclaiming over God's creations in terms that seem to underscore the comparative and seeming "nothingness of man" (see Mosiah 4:5, 11; Helaman 12:7; Moses 1:10). Certainly the vastness of God's creations can make us feel as if we are comparatively nothing; it caused dazzled Enoch to say to our loving Lord, "Yet thou art there" (Moses 7:30). But the reality is that we are children of God! We are of great worth!

Again, gospel perspectives are vital. Losing oneself means losing concern over getting credit; by knowing our true identity we need not be concerned about seeming anonymity. It likewise means losing our desire to be in the driver's seat; putting our shoulder to the wheel is enough.

It means that eagles meekly serve under sparrows—without worrying over comparative wingspans or plumage.

Losing oneself means yielding the substance of one's own agendum if it does not match the agendum of the Lord. It means losing the elements of our leadership style which are not consistent with His. (It is, after all, easier to be a character than to have character.)

There are affirmative things which accompany the losing of self. One is greater caring for the needy. There are many who thirst not only for water or hunger not only for bread but also for the word of the Lord and for friendship. The needy include both the poor in substance and those who are poor as to needed support systems. Losing oneself brings more noticing of others. The more preoccupied we are, the more who will pass by us unnoticed (see Mormon 8:39). We should, then, be more mindful of others, as God is always mindful of man.

Losing oneself means keeping ourselves more spiritually intact; being "ready always" (1 Peter 3:15) so that we are able to help more. Self-denial means patience and humility in a crowd, in a queue, in a parking lot, or with a harassed clerk.

Being of good cheer may not halt or deflect the downpour of discouragement which is drenching others, but it is the unfolding of an umbrella and walking together under it.

Losing ourselves means being willing to go to Nineveh when we would much prefer to go to Tarshish (see Jonah 1:2–3).

Losing oneself means losing one's impulsiveness. Jesus told Peter to put up the sword (see John 18:11). He told Oliver Cowdery he had to make intellectual effort in order to receive revelation (D&C 9:8–9).

Losing ourselves means dropping our resistance to feedback so that we can grow faster, just as did meek and receptive Moses, the brother of Jared, Peter, and Joseph Smith.

The Ten Commandments (Exodus 20:1–17) focus on our relationships with God, self, parents, and neighbors. Further commandments add detail. In addition to honoring God, we are to honor our parents. We are to honor others. We are to esteem neighbors as ourselves (see Philippians 2:3; Mosiah 27:4; D&C 38:24). We honor God by surrendering to God, by giving away our sins—putting at His feet the old self, old baggage, old equipment, and so on. Doing this ensures our getting to know God, and it brings greater richness in all other relationships too.

On the other hand, a swollen self will resist denial and surrender and will almost automatically violate the Ten Commandments, whether by profaning God's name or by neglecting parents. A swollen self is not sensitive and submissive. It is demonstrably indifferent to the life needs of others and may even violate the sixth commandment, whether by actually slaying someone or by enslaving him—for example, with drugs.

A swollen self may exhibit carelessness about the property of another by stealing, defrauding, or "dealing falsely," thus violating the eighth commandment.

A swollen self may be tempted to sexually violate the sanctity and purity of another human, thus disobeying the seventh commandment.

A swollen self can be insensitive to the reputation of others by defaming, libeling, whispering innuendos, or being a "tale bearer," thus violating the ninth commandment.

A swollen self can look at a person or a thing and say "I need it, so I will take it, it is mine"! If he cannot take it, he probably will covet it intensely.

The case of Cain is instructive. Apparently as he reached the age described as that in which an individual "became for himself" (3 Nephi 1:29) "Cain hearkened not [to his parents], saying: Who is the Lord that I should know him?" Later, when his less-than-best offering was not accepted by the Lord, he became "wroth," listening neither to the Lord nor to Abel, whose offering, he told the Lord, "thou didst accept and not mine." Cain said he was "tempted because of [his] brother's flocks." After killing Abel, he declared, "I am free," realizing that his brother's flocks were now his. Coveting preceded murdering, but Cain's unhearkening self preceded all else. (See Moses 5:16–38.)

The swollen self can, of course, be temporarily cut down to size by circumstances, as Laman and Lemuel demonstrated, but it cannot be finally shrunken except by submissiveness to the commandments of God. The giving away of our sins means that our souls can thereafter be genuinely enlarged "without hypocrisy, and without guile" (D&C 121:42).

So much of our maturing—whether avoiding being offended, being disappointed, being discouraged, feeling neglected, feeling unappreciated and unheeded—consists of shifting the emphasis from meeting "my" needs to meeting those of others. More accurately still, however, the eye that is single sees—for the first time—what one's own needs really are! We gain a fresh view and can change accordingly.

Losing our lives for Christ's sake really means exploring and discovering things about ourselves and others which we have never known. In that journey we will have the best of guides. This journey can easily be refused, however. We can loiter about in the spa of selfishness.

To gain the whole world indulgently causes an individual finally to lose his soul and to become a "castaway" (1 Corinthians 9:27). What then of worthwhile achievements which gain comparative trifles—so much less than the whole world?

An attorney may neglect weightier, spiritual things in order to labor legitimately for several years to lower his corporation's taxes by two percent.

A professor may neglect his family to publish a book which at last is chosen by an academic jury as a class text.

A scientist may let his marriage wither and perish while he comes up with a new process which will increase the lifespan of stored food.

These lesser labors are legitimate accomplishments. Commendable self-discipline has been involved, which is a portable, spiritual quality.

But Jesus pleads with us to develop a sense of proportion, lest we "strain at a gnat, and swallow a camel" (Matthew 23:24). On the two great commandments, said He, all the law and the prophets hang (see Matthew 22:40). Furthermore, amid many spiritual duties, there are some things that are "of the most worth," the "weightier matters" (D&C 15:4-6; Matthew 23:23).

This sense of proportion is one of the great benefits of seeing with the eye single. The eye single is not fooled by fancyness into ignoring plainness. Brigham Young reminded us, for instance, that many of the things which seem so plain to us in the gospel are actually the mysteries.

> If you could see things as they are, you would know that the whole plan of salvation, and all the revelations ever given to man on the earth are as plain as would be the remarks of an Elder, were he to stand here and talk about our every day business.... You may now be inclined to say, "O, this is too simple and child-like, we wish to hear the mysteries of the kingdoms of the Gods who have existed from eternity, and of all the kingdoms in which they will dwell; we desire to have these things portrayed to our understandings." Allow me to inform you that you are in the midst of it all now. (*Journal of Discourses* 3:336.)

What seems so plain—keeping the commandments in one's daily life—is "it!" There is not something else of a higher order which we are supposed to be doing instead.

This spiritual reality may seem unspectacular, even ordinary, especially if one assumes that some more important and more glamorous chore awaits beyond the horizon. To keep the commandments and to honor our covenants—whether one is a cashier at a grocery checkout counter, a neurosurgeon, an automotive mechanic, or a government official—is what matters, daily and eternally (see Luke 9:23). Each individual is to give away his sins, to deny himself, to lose himself, and then to find himself and full and everlasting joy.

When other things push away or prevent the doing of these simple, seemingly ordinary things, we are in deep trouble—especially when we no longer realize what the real things are!

So it is that this restored work not only involves the things of eternity but is also drenched in daily significance. True disciples, for instance, would be consistent environmentalists—caring both about maintaining the spiritual health of a marriage and preserving a rain forest; caring about preserving the nurturing capacity of a family as well as providing a healthy supply of air and water; caring for both the prevention and the treatment of the miseries caused by the diseases of transgression.

Adam and Eve were to "dress the garden," not exploit it. Like them, we are to keep the commandments, so that we can enjoy all the resources God has given us, resources described as "enough and to spare" (D&C 104:17), if we use and husband them wisely.

Given the flood of light and its fresh view, one's personal life is to be constantly pursued across the full range of symmetrical Christian virtues. One could be a great missionary through sharing the gospel but still be slack in doing needed civic chores. One can perform impressive civic chores yet be a failure within his own family (see 1 Samuel 2:12; 3:13). One may appropriately and publicly celebrate beauty yet lack reverence for other aspects of the divine.

Commendable generosity in one thing does not reduce our accountability for smallness of soul in another. Remember "one thing thou lackest" (Mark 10:21).

Aside from the consideration of proper balance in our lives, those who make commendable contributions may in one sense have already received their recognition and reward—here and now (see Matthew 6:2, 5, 16). This may be just as well, for some honors—justifiable enough here—would be embarrassing to receive later in a celestial setting.

Even worthy, mortal roles can entrap us. As we make contributions, these often draw to us applause, audiences, and even loyal constituencies. Recognition can turn our heads and we can lose the fresh view by being diverted from the need to become more like meek Jesus.

Speaking of contributions, it is better to be sure to do a few things than to do nothing. Moreover, even if we are personally inconsistent, others are still blessed personally by our genuine contributions.

There are, for each of us, mote and beam inconsistencies to be "given away"!

Losing ourselves includes a willingness to witness for Jesus, as this insightful translation of Joseph Smith's makes clear:

> But he who denieth me before men, shall be denied before the angels of God.
>
> Now his disciples knew that he said this, because they had spoken evil against him before the people; for they were afraid to confess him before men.
>
> And they reasoned among themselves, saying, He knoweth our hearts, and he speaketh to our condemnation, and we shall not be forgiven. But he answered them, and said unto them,
>
> Whosoever shall speak a word against the Son of Man, and repenteth, it shall be forgiven him; but unto him who blasphemeth against the Holy Ghost, it shall not be forgiven him. (JST, Luke 12:9–12.)

Jesus thus gave reassurance to His anxious disciples who apparently had not publicly confessed His name sufficiently. Yet there was hope, if they repented. This is another example of how repentance can bring about real and needed changes in our lives.

One of the most difficult things for us to "give away" is our Martha-like anxiety, our being conscientiously "careful and troubled about many things" (Luke 10:41). Such worrying and working may even make us feel approved, so that the things of the moment come to dominate the things of eternity. The meal Martha was busily and conscientiously preparing was soon eaten and forgotten. Mary, instead, had "chosen that good part," which would not be taken from her; she had a sense of proportion.

Some of the time, therefore, as with Martha, we murmur because we are focused on the wrong things through lack of perspective. Laman and Lemuel lacked gospel perspective, so they grumbled over one thing or another (see 1 Nephi 2:12).

Martha-like anxiety also expresses itself in our hurrying, even in good causes. Rushing, we find the red traffic light on the way to an important meeting. A fuse goes out, halting the carefully prepared entertainment of guests. When buying a gift for someone in need, we unexpectedly encounter a long line. Doesn't God know we are in a hurry! Doesn't He realize we are only hurrying in order to do something that is good! Thus we can be "anxiously engaged" in a "good cause" but fail to keep things in perspective, having not chosen "that good part."

When genuine frustrations come along, we are still urged to bear them with good cheer and with patience (see Mosiah 24:15). Patience is for coping with unmet expectations, since the way not only is strait and narrow but also lacks a smooth surface.

A new layer of experience cannot be laid down without our feeling its weight and its immediacy. New cares, therefore, so soon cover the old, as the present muffles the past. For instance, a much-needed but unexpected check arrives in time to ease financial worries, and the next day the car is found to need a new transmission. Or children and grandchildren arrive safely after a long and anxious journey and are tucked away safely in one's household, and then the baby cries all night.

"Now" is "now." Hence it is so easy to say of our best blessings, "That was then and this is now." The very nature of our five senses—of hearing, of seeing, of smelling, of touching, of tasting—focuses us on now. How does one say to the eye, "Don't receive the next impression"? or to the ear, "Ignore that incoming sound"?

One of the functions of the sixth sense is to balance yesterday, today, and tomorrow with spiritual remembrance.

There is not much space in this life for reveries. Instead, the "old roomers," the cares of the world, quickly move back in, evicting bliss and sometimes even memories of blessings.

Jesus issued pointed words to sign-seeking hypocrites who could "discern the face of the sky" but nevertheless did "not discern the signs of the times" (Matthew 16:3). They could forecast the local weather for the next brief moment but could not see the enveloping things of deeper import! Yet they wanted a sign from heaven, when there were signs all about them which they simply could not discern! The weather presses itself daily upon us, but it is always changing and passing; the weather is proximate, however, not ultimate.

When we have an eye single to God's glory, there is no room for other consuming causes. Yes, we are to be anxiously engaged in good causes, but all good causes are actually subsets of God's great cause—to bring to pass the immortality and eternal life of man (see Moses 1:39; Moroni 7:28). Moreover, just after the words indicating that we are to be "anxiously engaged" in a good cause of our own free will, we are reminded that we must obey the commandments (see D&C 58:30).

We desperately need the perspective which comes from an eye single. Such an eye is focused. It is not blurred at the edges. It also has real depth perception. It sees both the things close at hand (the needs of our own families) and things distant (the needs of the human family). An eye single can identify the returning prodigal while he is "yet a great way off," or it can spot a very distant tiny cloud that signals rescuing rain (see Luke 15:20; 1 Kings 18:44).

The natural man's ways are not God's ways, in large measure because we lack His eyes. We lack the focused vision that is provided by an "eye single" only when our "minds become single to God" and to his work and glory (D&C 59:1; 88:68).

God sees as if in an "eternal now." We myopic mortals tend to think our present sample is the total sample—"all things continue as they were from the beginning" (2 Peter 3:4).

The "eye single" is minus the motes and beams of sin, and signifies being "pure and undimmed by sin" (James E. Talmage, *Jesus the Christ* [Salt Lake City: Deseret Book, 1962], p. 243).

The Perfect Example is ever before us. Our unique Lord can thus encourage us. Furthermore, as to the giving away of our sins, there is only one who can take them in order that we might not suffer needlessly. But there is more! He who has done so much for us would also have us become more like Him!

Chapter Seven

"THERE IS NONE LIKE UNTO THE LORD"

The fact that Jesus is actually to be our Exemplar is made abundantly and directly clear, especially in the restored gospel's wonderful flood of light. This requirement is not something to be brushed aside. Indeed, it cannot be, when we have the fresh view of reality.

For I have given you an example, that ye should do as I have done to you (John 13:15).

Jesus Christ [shows] forth all longsuffering, for a pattern to them which should hereafter believe on him to life everlasting (1 Timothy 1:16).

Christ also suffered for us, leaving us an example, that ye should follow his steps (1 Peter 2:21).

And again, it showeth unto the children of men the straitness of the path, and the narrowness of the gate, by which they should enter, he having set the example before them (2 Nephi 31:9).

Verily, verily, I say unto you, this is my gospel; and ye know the things that ye must do in my church; for the works which ye have seen me do that shall ye also do; for that which ye have seen me do even that shall ye do (3 Nephi 27:21).

Behold I am the light; I have set an example for you (3 Nephi 18:16).

Each of us plays various roles in family, Church, community, business, education, and so forth. Though we have differing needs, we have in common the need to focus on all Christ's qualities, especially those which individually we most need to develop more fully, for "he that saith he abideth in him ought himself also so to walk, even as he walked" (1 John 2:6).

In the quietude of individual contemplation of Christ's qualities we will find much customized counsel. In some cases it may be pointed, as it was for the rich, righteous young man who queried Jesus about what more he needed to do to obtain eternal life. "Then Jesus beholding him loved him, and said unto him, One thing thou lackest: go thy way, sell whatsoever thou hast, and give to the poor, and thou shalt have treasure in heaven: and come, take up the cross, and follow me. And he was sad at that saying, and went away grieved: for he had great possessions." (Mark 10:21-22.)

We can, of course, stop short and merely adopt a few techniques illustrated by the Savior. But unless we emulate Him as completely as we can, we will have deprived ourselves of the great model. Moreover, our emulation is to be of both style and substance. God's love underwrites his listening, for instance. Can we conceive of a God who is a nonlistener? Or who is lacking in power? Or who is unwilling to assert Himself on an issue of principle? As we become more like Him it will take place in both attributes and actions.

Even attempting merely to list the qualities of Jesus Christ will fall short, to say nothing of attempting to describe those marvelous qualities.

Underlying the striking patterns of leadership are many qualities of the Master Leader, among which are these few:

1. In both premortality and mortality Jesus prepared Himself superbly.
2. On earth as in heaven, He cared totally about the Father's cause and was "anxiously engaged" in it. There was no sin in Him, nor ambivalence either. Never was an eye as single nor an individual thereby so filled with light.
3. He cared about His followers, loving them with a perfect love. He denied Himself any wrong things and "lost" Himself in service to all mankind. Eventually, His joy was full.
4. He exemplified for His followers what manner of individuals they could and should become.
5. He taught His followers specifically, individually, and effectively.
6. He gave His followers feedback but did so while "speaking the truth in love" (Ephesians 4:15).
7. He stayed ever close to Heavenly Father, giving temptations "no heed" (D&C 20:22).
8. He constantly gave all glory to the Father (see Moses 4:2; D&C 19:19).
9. He taught correct principles, including the principle that we have responsibility for ourselves as we choose our words, thoughts, and actions.
10. He suffered terribly, but He is also long-suffering as to His patience and redemptiveness toward us.
11. He wisely selected others to their various roles, having foreordained some long ago, whom He also "called and prepared" (Alma 13:2–3).
12. He used time wisely, including precious teaching moments.
13. He helped his followers to remember truths and to learn from relevant experiences.
14. He gave the greatest answers to the most searching queries, but He also asked inspired and productive questions.

Granted, we lack Jesus' immense knowledge, for "neither could he be taught; for he needed not that any man should teach him" (JST, Matthew 3:25). Granted, too, even though we mortals are kinsmen eternally, our "here and now" relationships often involve only short-term associations. Moreover, we do not always choose those with whom we work. Even so, all the principles and patterns of Jesus' leadership are crucial for us to understand and to apply.

Christ blended humility with His divinity. An example is his openly acknowledging, "My doctrine is not mine, but his that sent me" (John 7:16). Also, "Be ye therefore perfect, even as your Father which is in heaven is perfect" (Matthew 5:48).

He continued to teach correct principles, blending accuracy and modesty, even after He was perfected and resurrected. "Therefore I would that ye should be perfect even as I, or your Father who is in heaven is perfect" (3 Nephi 12:48). "Therefore, what manner of men ought ye to be? Verily I say unto you, even as I am" (3 Nephi 27:27).

This inclusion of Himself as a model shows His devotion to truth even amid His marvelous meekness. He desires us to become "finished" and "completed."

What a student-son He had been!

"Then answered Jesus and said unto them, Verily, verily, I say unto you, The Son can do nothing of himself, but what he seeth the Father do: for what things soever he doeth, these also doeth the Son likewise" (John 5:19). By following the Father's example, then, Jesus became perfected in His attributes of love, mercy, patience, meekness, knowledge, truth, judgment, and so forth. Though we lack many qualities, we have been directed to become more like Him in each of those attributes. Obviously the way for *us* to achieve perfection is to follow *His* example.

The stunning doctrines of the Restoration tell us of our own individual beginnings and also of our possibilities in eternity—of pedigrees and possibilities! We must not be lulled or dulled simply because, meanwhile, we are so imperfect. Nor should we rationalize our responsibilities simply because we are often in short-term relationships with other people. The hungry or thirsty stranger, Jesus said, represents more than himself or herself (see Matthew 25:31–46).

We are accountable for doing our part in all relationships and for providing what leadership, service, and influence we can. Those within our circles of influence constitute our present sample of humanity; they are neither mere functionaries nor strangers in a transit lounge.

Jesus was a principle-centered leader but also a people-centered leader. Jesus spoke "the truth in love" (Ephesians 4:15), both correcting and commending. As noted, during the space of a three-hour visit with the Lord the admirable brother of Jared was reproved for not remembering to be sufficiently prayerful (see Ether 2:14). Yet later Jesus warmly commended this same prophet by saying, "Never has man believed in me as thou hast" (Ether 3:15).

Unlike Jesus, sometimes we are so concerned with our own feelings and those of others that we subordinate principles to feelings, or vice versa! Hence we often do too little both of correcting and of commending.

Joseph Smith knew what it was to be corrected by the Lord (see D&C 10:1-3). So did Oliver Cowdery (see D&C 9:7). Their reproofs were not vague but very specific: the Prophet Joseph Smith's for not following original instructions concerning the Book of Mormon manuscript, and Oliver Cowdery's for not continuing as he had commenced and for thinking he merely needed to ask for revelations without making intellectual effort.

Jesus tutored Peter in a highly individualistic way, mixing reproof ("Put up again thy sword"—Matthew 26:52) and commendation ("Blessed art thou . . . flesh and blood hath not revealed it unto thee . . ."—Matthew 16:17). Peter overreacted to one reproof, declaring, "Lord, not my feet only, but also my hands and my head" (John 13:8-10).

The correct manner and motivation for reproof are indicated in Doctrine and Covenants 121:43. In practice, however, when we undertake to reprove we frequently are prompted not by the Holy Ghost but by ego. Moreover, we often fail to reprove "betimes," meaning speedily and *early on.* Time can harden feelings as surely as the sun bakes wet clay.

Jesus was willing to provide tutorials in one-on-one audiences with some of His followers. Such personalized help can be especially nourishing in the tenderest and most needful moments. For instance, Christ stood by imprisoned Paul in the night to cheer the Apostle and also to call him to Rome (see Acts 23:11). One cannot help but wonder, when Shadrach, Meshach, and Abednego were in the fiery furnace, if it might not have been the Lord Himself who was the fourth figure in that fiery furnace (see Daniel 3:25).

The Lord used such salutatory and tutorial tenderness, as we read in his words to Moses and Joseph Smith:

> And, behold, thou art *my son*; wherefore look, and I will show thee the workmanship of mine hands. . . .
> And I have a work for thee, Moses, *my son*; and thou art in the similitude of mine Only Begotten. . . .
> And now, behold, this one thing I show unto thee, Moses, *my son*; for thou art in the world, and now I show it unto thee. (Moses 1:4, 6–7, italics added.)

> *My son*, peace be unto thy soul; thine adversity and thine afflictions shall be but a small moment; . . . (D&C 121:7, italics added).

> Know thou, *my son*, that all these things shall give thee experience, and shall be for thy good (D&C 122:7, italics added).

The Lord's being so near at hand was underscored by Enoch's exclamation about our Lord's many creations amid the expanses of space: "Yet thou art there" (Moses 7:30).

There are dozens of such highly personalized reassurances in the scriptures. Examples are the Lord's words to Abraham and to Jeremiah, which encouraged them by giving them precious, personal perspective:

> Before I formed thee in the belly I knew thee; and before thou camest forth out of the womb I sanctified thee, and I ordained thee a prophet unto the nations (Jeremiah 1:5).

And God saw these souls that they were good, and he stood in the midst of them, and he said: These I will make my rulers; for he stood among those that were spirits, and he saw that they were good; and he said unto me: Abraham, thou art one of them; thou wast chosen before thou wast born (Abraham 3:23).

Divine praise was given to a humble Roman centurion: "I have not found so great faith, no, not in Israel" (Matthew 8:10).

Jesus prophesied in ways that allowed later remembrance to occur: "Verily I say unto you, That this night, before the cock crow. . . ." (Matthew 26:34); and "This he said, signifying by what death [Peter] should die" (John 12:33). A developing faith in Jesus Christ is much aided by the provision of spiritual evidence of His foreseeing and individualizing.

To the humble woman of Samaria who knew that the Messiah was to come, Jesus made a simple declaration—"I that speak unto thee am he" (John 4:26)—in confirming His divinity, which He withheld from others, including the inquiring but powerful Pilate.

Aaron, who may have yielded to the crowd during the golden calf episode, was nevertheless honored later by having the lesser priesthood named after him and his seed "throughout all their generations" (Exodus 32:2–6; D&C 84:18). Jesus lifts us up in a world which so often puts people down.

Though sometimes sternly tutored, Peter was honored as the chief Apostle, and with James and John he became the means whereby the apostleship was restored to the Prophet Joseph Smith (see D&C 128:20).

All of these and other examples combine to let us know that Jesus provides forgiving hope for His serious and sincere followers. That hope was extended even to the woman who was taken in adultery, for Jesus' focus was on her and not on the crowd. In fact, he confronted the crowd by inviting any who were without sin to cast the first stone. Yet Jesus acted redemptively, not permissively, telling the woman to "go, and sin no more." (John 8:1–11.)

Jesus attended to important details, such as the Nephite failure to record the prophecy of Samuel, the Lamanite, about the general resurrection following Jesus' resurrection (3 Nephi 23:9–13; see also Matthew 27:52–53). The editorial reproof was pointed but not overdone.

The great David had it "in [his] mind" to build a temple to the Lord, but because he had "shed much blood" he was not the man to do it, and instead it was to be done by Solomon (see 1 Chronicles 22:7–9). The Lord was direct with David as to the reason for the restraint, but His love for David did not cease, even though the assignment to build a glorious temple was given to another.

Jesus customized His counsel while simultaneously teaching great, general principles.

Even Thomas (who needed to see in order to believe) was still told that he was blessed. Then the Savior taught a general principle: "Blessed are they that have not seen, and yet have believed." That principle was soon amplified to the Nephites: Blessed are they who see and believe, but "more blessed are they who shall believe in your words because that ye shall testify that ye have seen me." (John 20:24–29; 3 Nephi 12:1–2.)

After the miracle of the loaves and fishes, the details of which apparently were soon forgotten by the Apostles, Jesus reproved them by using remembrance, asking them to recall how many baskets of leftovers had been picked up (see Matthew 16:6–12). Teaching in the present can be enriched by remembrance of previous lessons.

As a result of Jesus' teaching to a formerly legalistic Paul, the Apostle to the Gentiles, the latter was able to write his powerful verses on charity (see 1 Corinthians 13). Paul also wrote about the importance of "speaking the truth in love" (Ephesians 4:15).

Jesus, meek and lowly, encourages us to learn of Him and His meekness by taking His yoke upon us so that, better sensing such weight, we too might be meek and lowly.

Too many times, if we look beneath a failure or ponder a situation we did not handle well, we will find that our ego was extruding, a situation ranging from talking too much to putting someone else down. Or that we showed insufficient love, displayed in a range from our casualness on the one hand to our failure to commend or correct on the other.

Jesus was unconcerned with His personal visibility or His ascendancy. He deliberately descended below all. Contrariwise, the scriptures as well as secular history are full of examples of people for whom ego trips became life's only journey.

> Truly, to be Prime Minister was fun but to be Prime Minister and Lloyd George at one and the same time was very heaven!
>
> The time would eventually come when he would cease to marvel at the position in which he found himself and regard the adulation of the mob as no more than his rightful due. The cheerful good humour would slowly dissolve into a colossal egotism. (Peter Rowland, *Lloyd George* [London: Barrie and Jenkins, 1975], p. 376.)

Some find themselves "needing acclaim as a man with a goiter needs iodine" (Ted Morgan, *Churchill* [New York: Simon and Schuster, 1982], p. 434). In fact, Brooks Adams observed that "the effect of power and publicity on all men is the aggravation of self, a sort of tumor that ends by killing the victim's sympathies" (Henry Brooks Adams, p. 776, quoted in John Bartlett, comp. *Familiar Quotations*, 14th ed. [New York: Macmillan, 1968], p. 776).

How different is Jesus! Truly "there is none like unto the Lord" (Exodus 8:10). Yet "the world, because of their iniquity, shall judge him to be a thing of naught; wherefore they scourge him, and he suffereth it; and they smite him, and he suffereth it. Yea, they spit upon him, and he suffereth it, because of his loving kindness and his long-suffering towards the children of men." (1 Nephi 19:9.)

Even after treading the winepress alone (see D&C 76:107), which ended in His stunning personal triumph and in the greatest victory ever, majestic Jesus meekly declared, "Glory be to the Father"! (D&C 19:19.) This should not surprise us. In the premortal world Jesus meekly volunteered to be our Savior,

saying, "Father, thy will be done, and the glory be thine forever" (Moses 4:2). Jesus was ever true to His word.

In contrast to Jesus' meekness, most of us have keen and
continuing concerns about status. There were, by way of example, those who had deep concern that Moses or Nephi not
"rule over them."

> Is it a small thing that thou hast brought us up out of a
> land that floweth with milk and honey, to kill us in the wil-
> derness, except thou make thyself altogether a prince over us?
> (Numbers 16:13.)

> And Laman said unto Lemuel and also unto the sons of
> Ishmael: Behold, let us slay our father, and also our brother
> Nephi, who has taken it upon him to be our ruler and our
> teacher, who are his elder brethren (1 Nephi 16:37).

> Yea, they did murmur against me, saying: Our younger
> brother thinks to rule over us; and we have had much trial
> because of him; wherefore, now let us slay him, that we may
> not be afflicted more because of his words. For behold, we will
> not have him to be our ruler; for it belongs unto us, who are
> the elder brethren, to rule over this people. (2 Nephi 5:3.)

Jesus not only gave the greatest answers to life's greatest
questions, but He also knew how to put especially productive
questions. Frequently His interrogatives carried with them
leadership lessons. "How is it that ye do not understand?" (Matthew 16:11–12) is a phrase used several times (see also Matthew
15:17). This was not an impatient complaint by Jesus, as it
might be if it came from us, but rather was His invitation to
ponder and to analyze. "Why do ye not understand my speech?
even because ye cannot hear my word" (John 8:43).

His salutation and questions were sometimes very personal,
whether to Saul, to Joseph Smith, or to Peter. "Saul, Saul, why
persecutest thou me?" (Acts 9:4.) Then there was the tender but
probing "Lovest thou me?" (John 21:15–17.)

In a most tender but teaching scene, reverential and ador-
ing Mary, at the feet of the resurrected Jesus, was constrained

—"Touch me not; for I am not yet ascended to my Father" (John 20:17). Jesus would not let Mary's expression of even the most devout and sincere adoration result in an error. He loves us too much to look the other way.

He loves even those who refuse His counsel, as in the case of the rich and righteous young man who had done all that he was supposed to do—yet "lacked" one thing (Mark 10:17–22).

Jesus' commendations are both personalized and specific. Hyrum Smith was commended for the "integrity" of his heart (D&C 124:15). Nathaniel was commended for being an Israelite "in whom is no guile" (John 1:47).

Is our praise, when we give it, both justified and specific enough?

Even in the less-attended-to episodes in holy scripture we find rich instruction and example from Jesus' leadership. For instance, He was able to forego recognition in the conversation with two of His disciples on the road to Emmaus. Instead, He taught them from the holy scriptures, deferring recognition.

We sometimes have difficulty in deferring recognition.

Jesus could not have done the things He did if He had been like some of us—fretting over dominion, fearing the criticism of the world, and seeking glory and praise. In contrast there was Lucifer, whose ascendancy was more important to him than our agency (see Moses 4:1, 3).

Though aware of them, Jesus was unperturbed by the comings and goings and the connivings of secular rulers such as Herod and Pilate. "And the same day Pilate and Herod were made friends together: for before they were at enmity between themselves" (Luke 23:12). They "made a deal," but were soon out of power. Jesus went forward with His eternal ministry, His cause being the cause of all mankind (see Moroni 7:28).

Jesus is the Master Leader not only because He is meek and lowly and thus can cope with irony and adversity but also because He counsels us correctly as to life's basics. One of these is that we are not to seek the things of this world. Instead we are to seek first to *build up* the kingdom of God and *to establish* His righteousness; and if we do this, all that we need will be added to us (JST, Matthew 6:38). In order to "seek first" we should first deny ourselves (Luke 9:23).

We are especially warned about the dangers of ingratitude, pride, riches, and power.

In so many ways we are told what manner of men and women we ought to become (see 3 Nephi 27:27). He commands us, "Settle this in your hearts, that ye will do the things which I shall teach, and command you" (JST, Luke 14:28). Through his prophets He pleads with us to become "settled" (Colossians 1:23).

There are several things which are typically difficult for us in daily life.

For example, it is difficult for us to let virtue garnish our thoughts unceasingly (D&C 121:45). Do we really expect it to be otherwise—complete with authorized recesses from righteousness?

It is easy for us to be offended, because "it must needs be that offences come" (Matthew 18:7). Yes, those who give offense are fully accountable, but especially "blessed is he, whosoever shall not be offended in me" (Matthew 11:6; see also 13:21).

It is difficult for us, when doing good, to avoid "pleasing ourselves" (Romans 15:1)—even if only by reflecting inwardly and favorably—or to resist adulation.

It is difficult not to grow weary of well doing (see Galatians 6:9). Jesus commended one prophet for his "unwearyingness" (Helaman 10:4–5).

It is difficult for us to be long-suffering with others, as God surely is with us (see Exodus 34:6; 2 Corinthians 6:6; 1 Peter 3:20).

It is difficult for us to speak in favor of one who deserves support but whom the crowd is against unjustifiably. Jesus befriended lepers and publicans, and rescued and counseled the beseiged, adulterous woman (see John 8:3–11).

It is difficult for us to put our hand to the plow without looking back; we are insufficiently "settled" spiritually.

It is difficult for us to be meek and lowly. Praise can turn our heads away from concentrating on the furrow to be plowed.

It is difficult for us to speak the truth in love (Ephesians 4:15).

It is difficult for us to respond to cutting truths, even when these lancing words make it possible to drain off pride (see 1 Nephi 16:2). Like Laman and Lemuel, we may mistake truth for anger.

It is difficult for us to endure aloneness even in a good cause.

Perhaps the most difficult of all is the task of balancing these important principles. How, for instance, does one balance speaking the truth in love on the one hand with being long-suffering on the other? How does one balance not doing things "to be seen of men" with avoiding hiding one's light under a bushel?

Thus we must have His Spirit to be with us, to show us not only all things we must do but how to do them with proper spiritual poise (see 2 Nephi 32:3).

Jesus did not act amiss. He always provided what was needed. He was always teaching and counseling. He did His work in a customized way. He knows his sheep and they follow Him (see John 10:27). Thus we see Him rescuing and emancipating a woman taken in adultery; providing a crowning ordinance for protesting Peter; declaring His divinity to a devout woman from Samaria; praising and healing for a centurion; diagnosing for Oliver Cowdery's failure but reassuring Oliver that he was not condemned; tutoring the Brother of Jared on how to build a barge; witnessing and restraining for Mary at the empty tomb; praising Peter; reassuring Jeremiah and Abraham. On and on the stunning list goes!

Thus God's ways as shown forth by the Son are vastly higher than man's ways (see Isaiah 55:8–9). And in terms of constancy and consistency, He is the same yesterday, and today, and forever (see Hebrews 13:8). We are at the mercy of our moods.

His view is universal. Ours is provincial.

He is selfless. We are selfish. He is perfection, we are imperfection. He lives in an "eternal now." We live in time and are concerned with daily things, including our daily bread. He has perfect remembrance. We are forgetful.

Whether in a micro or a macro mode, God is "able to do [His] own work." Parting the Red Sea for ancient Israel was easy for Him who, centuries before, had brought to pass the parting or dividing of the earth's oceans and continents (see Genesis 10:25; 1 Chronicles 1:19; D&C 133:24).

God lets us choose, just as He allowed Cain to think, erroneously, that he was "free" after he had slain his brother Abel (see Moses 5:33). He likewise allowed some ancient Jews to engage in "looking beyond the mark" (Jacob 4:14).

He emancipated ancient Israel from Egypt. He has tilted the earth just right and moves it in orbit in such a way that we have seasons. He also reminds us that there can be "seasons" in our own lives (Ecclesiastes 3:1).

On Sinai He wrote on tablets for all mankind the words of the Ten Commandments. To those open to promptings, He causes the individual burning of the bosom to affirm the truthfulness of certain things.

As we consider His long-suffering, His timing, His purposes, and His omniscience, the best and only way to become like Him is as a result of our own willing and consistent pattern of choices, but not because He has intimidated us.

Those of us who are acquainted with the still, small voice are personal witnesses to His micro-management. We are not surprised, therefore, that He who foresaw that certain manuscript pages of the Book of Mormon would be lost had centuries before made ample provision for the work to go forward just the same (see headings to Doctrine and Covenants sections 3 and 10; 1 Nephi 9:5–6; Words of Mormon 1:5–7; Mormon 8).

Those striving to follow the Savior know of the reality of God's marvelous capacity because, from time to time, we too are able to do some of His work. Inadequate as we are, He uses us—sometimes well beyond our known capacity. And we know it and witness that it is so! For this, however, we should give to Him all the honor, praise, and glory! We should not, of course, boast of ourselves, but only of Him. (See Alma 26:12, 35-36.)

Not only do we have perfect Jesus as our ultimate Exemplar, but also His servants, the men and women of God, are proximate examples. Though imperfect, these individuals mirror significantly in their lives qualities perfected in the Master. Enoch, as he became better and better informed, found his empathy growing until figuratively "his heart swelled wide as eternity" (Moses 7:41). Much inspiration can come to us from our companions in the journey of discipleship. Therefore the concept of believers being "compassed about with so great a cloud of witnesses" (Hebrews 12:1) is to be appreciated not only in terms of witnesses from antiquity such as Abel, Enoch, and Noah but also by the way in which the Lord's modern disciples likewise have sufficient faith in the Lord to mirror His qualities in their lives.

By citing only a few qualities possessed by a few First Presidency members of the recent past one can see how each of these "witnesses" joins the compassing cloud.

President Joseph Fielding Smith was not only a prophet who taught the whole Church but he also taught his considerable posterity especially well. Like Lehi, he was anxious "that [his] family should partake" (1 Nephi 8:12). To the very end of his mortality, one saw in President Smith the seriousness of his own discipleship, including his persistent desire to honor his covenants. Though seemingly stern, President Smith was especially merciful. His posterity is a tribute to him not only as a prophet but also as a father, a grandfather, and a great-grandfather.

President Harold B. Lee, so conscious of Jesus' example, almost never ceased teaching, refusing to let a teaching moment pass unused.

As a Regional Representative, the author once accompanied President Lee to a stake reorganization. In the course of the interviews a spiritual experience occurred showing how the one called had unmistakable foreknowledge of the call. Ever the teacher, President Lee put his hand on my thigh and said simply, "You see, Neal, why it is so important for us to operate under the direction of the Spirit in doing this work?" It was a lesson never to be forgotten, because the teacher went the second mile to ensure that it would be so!

He was able to squeeze insights and lessons out of experiences and episodes which were compressed into small timeframes. President Lee did not have to go through prolonged experience in order to learn the lessons or gain the useful insights.

Being secure spiritually, he was unthreatened by those of the world who were presumed to know more than he. Being grounded and rooted in strategic truths, he invited and considered tactical insights from a surprising variety of sources.

President Spencer W. Kimball exhibited the same "unwearyingness" as the Lord commended in Nephi (Helaman 10:4–5). One of the author's last real conversations with President Kimball included his wistful comment concerning his ministry: "I should have done more!" How he could have done more none of us knows, but this comment is indicative of his unwearyingness. He endured so well the unusual number of afflictions life placed upon him while serving so many so incessantly.

He esteemed all people alike (see Mosiah 23:7; 27:4). He was not afraid of his moment in history (Helaman 7:9). He knew that his appointed days were his days and he used them well.

President N. Eldon Tanner also endured well, saying that the Lord "had never said it would be easy." President Tanner had the meekness which permitted him to advance an idea and then let it have a life of its own rather than oversponsor it with his immense personal prestige in order to give it some advantage in the arena of decision making. In years of association with him, the author remembers only once—and that was a brief and modest reference—when he mentioned his high-level experience in Canada in provincial government and in constructing the trans-Canada pipeline. A lesser man would have burdened colleagues with "Back when I was. . . ."

President Tanner never multiplied words, as was evidenced when, a few hours before he died, he gave his gathered family members a simple, powerful final sermonette the gist of which was: "Love one another, do not find fault with each other, and always forgive one another, always take counsel from the leaders of the Church and follow them diligently." (Personal account as related by his daughter, Ruth.)

President Romney also was meek and likewise endured well. He had that quiet confidence that goes with being "settled in his heart" (JST, Luke 14:28). He was so settled that he sometimes meekly remarked that he genuinely felt sorry for the critics and enemies of the Church, because in spite of them this work would inevitably triumph. His self-effacing sense of humor was possible because, being unconcerned with self, he had time to notice incongruities and ironies. The twinkle in his eyes reflected flashes from a soul "filled with light" and faith.

Each of us is blessed with his own cloud of affirming witnesses. Their leadership status, of course, matters little. It is what they transmitted that we cherish! If we but knew how anxious the Lord is for us to be more conscious and remembering of all those who compose our clouds of witnesses!

He also is anxious for us to be more aware that as members of His kingdom we are to be lights. As a major example, temple-worthy Church members do not fully understand how crucial they really are to all mankind. Jesus' words to his New Testament audience about salt and savor can be conjoined with His declarations in latter-day scriptures in this revealed way: "When men are called unto mine everlasting gospel, and covenant with an everlasting covenant, they are accounted as the salt of the earth and the savor of men" (D&C 101:39). Such individuals are "set to be a light unto the world, and to be the saviors of men" (D&C 103:9).

If those comparatively few people who have made temple covenants do not keep those covenants, what will happen then? The world does not understand this, but we should.

Modern temples relate us to things which are very ancient. Indeed, the holy temples tell us of things "plain and precious" —things lost for centuries which have now been restored—and part the curtains both to antiquity and to eternity.

Temples are designed not only to endow and to seal us but

also to refine us. The Second Book of Esdras, an apocryphal work, says: "The Most High made this world for the sake of many, but the world to come, for the sake of few. . . . The earth . . . produces much more clay from which earthenware is made, but little dust from which gold comes." (2 Esdras 8:1–3.) (Edgar J. Goodspeed, trans., *The Apochrypha: An American Translation* [New York: Vintage Books, 1959], p. 73.)

God seeks in so many ways to consecrate the events in our lives for the welfare of our souls, and we should even pray to Him that whatever we undertake to perform will be finally consecrated to that end (see 2 Nephi 32:9). Father Lehi prayed over the afflictions his son Jacob had known, including "the rudeness of thy brethren." Lehi asked that God "would consecrate [Jacob's] afflictions for [his] gain." (2 Nephi 2:1, 2.) Jacob doubtless denied himself reciprocal anger at Laman and Lemuel. Additionally, having lost himself, Jacob later found himself to be a poet prophet!

How could one so see life and act in this way without the gospel view of God, self, others, and the universe that comes with the Restoration's wonderful flood of light?

Our Father is truly anxious that our experiences, our performances, and even our afflictions move us forward spiritually. The moments of suffering may be our greatest moments, though at the time we would gladly forego them.

In describing His expansive Messianic mission summationally, Jesus has focused on His crowning moments of suffering. His great atoning and rescuing act is the essence of His gospel, as he told the Nephites,

> Behold I have given unto you my gospel, and *this is the gospel* which I have given unto you—that I came into the world to do the will of my Father, because my Father sent me.
>
> And my Father sent me that I might be lifted up upon the cross; and after that I had been lifted up upon the cross, that I might draw all men unto me, that as I have been lifted up by men even so should men be lifted up by the Father, to stand before me, to be judged of their works, whether they be good or whether they be evil. (3 Nephi 27:13–14, italics added.)

His further post-resurrection declarations about the Atonement correlate fully with the above summations:

> And behold, I am the light and the life of the world; and I have drunk out of that bitter cup which the Father hath given me, and have glorified the Father in taking upon me the sins of the world, in the which I have suffered the will of the Father in all things from the beginning (3 Nephi 11:11).

> Which suffering caused myself, even God, the greatest of all, to tremble because of pain, and to bleed at every pore, and to suffer both body and spirit—and would that I might not drink the bitter cup, and shrink—
>
> Nevertheless, glory be to the Father, and I partook and finished my preparations unto the children of men. (D&C 19:18–19.)

Many centuries after the Savior's declarations to the Nephites, the divine summation was much the same:

> And *this is the gospel*, the glad tidings, which the voice out of the heavens bore record unto us—
>
> That he came into the world, even Jesus, to be crucified for the world, and to bear the sins of the world, and to sanctify the world, and to cleanse it from all unrighteousness (D&C 76:40–41; italics added).

Jesus has described His restored gospel as constituting the "glad tidings" (D&C 31:3). Those joyous tidings have come to us by means of a "miraculous miracle."

What greater message could mortals hear? What more stunning words affirming life's meaning?

Surely "there is none like unto the Lord" (Exodus 8:10). And He actually asks us to strive to become more like Him. Of all possible goals, "there is none like" that one!

And, most important, He actually beckons us to come and live with Him forever! Of all possible invitations, "there is none like" that one!

Subject Index

Scripture Index

BOOK OF MORMON

DOCTRINE AND COVENANTS